CAN YOU? YES....

NILESH KUMAR AGARWAL

Made with ❤ on the Notion Press Platform
www.notionpress.com

Contents

Foreword   *v*

   1. Chapter 1   1

Foreword

Indian mythological author Nilesh Kumar Agarwal has been awarded for his contribution as an outstanding author by ICONS OF ASIA 2022. The author accepted the award at a ceremony in Delhi at Hotel Radisson BLU Dwarka. Nilesh Kumar Agarwal said he was "humbled and deeply honoured" to receive the recognition given by Global Empire Events. The distinguished award celebrates leaders in their field who demonstrate commitment to social change and reflect passion for building a strong society.

He was one of the honorees this year, who also included Speaker of the House Lord Diljit Rana (Member of Parliament – House of Lords, UK), Mrs. Shabeena Sultana (Honorary Consul of the Republic of Tunisia), Nawab Mir Nasir Ali Khan (Honorary Consul of Republic of Kazakhstan for Telangana

& Andhra Pradesh,India), Mr. Deepak Singh (Cultural Ambassador of Seychelles, Government of Seychelles), Shree Prashant Mukund Das an Spiritual Guide & Bhagavatam Katha Speaker.

The award is given to a writer whose work can be compared to that of other authors, suggesting that figures in Nilesh Kumar Agarwal's own work such as Indian traditions and their scientific reasons, Kabir couplets and ramayana, Essence of all religions are expected, by the judges at least, to have the enduring appeal of this award. This award is given annually to authors whose work is recognised around the globe. A statement from the organisation said: "Since his rise as an author, Nilesh Kumar Agarwal has used his talents and stature as a writer to fight inequality among people regarding different religions on both a local and global level.

Nilesh Kumar Agarwal is the founder of the non-profit-making organisation Nilesh Staallion Foundation, which supports humans and animals medically though crowdfunding. He had also done a mythological show with Radio City named "Ramayana Rehsaya" which was aired on Dussehra 2021 voiced by Madhushree Bhattacharya, a famous bollywood singer.

In his acceptance speech Nilesh Kumar Agarwal said: "I count this one of the highest honours I've ever been given. Also, I'm deeply honoured to receive this award and humbled that my work has been recognised as having moral value by an organisation I so admire," He expressed his pride at having been chosen to receive the award.

On 22nd September 2022, Nilesh Kumar Agarwal was awarded for his contribution as an outstanding author. He accepted the esteemed award from the Head of ISCKON, Dwarka. Mr. Prashant Mukund Das a Spiritual Guide & Bhagavatam Katha Speaker. He is associated with ISCKON from last 15 years and a great Preacher of vedic scriptures worldwide.

It is a special award held by Global Empire events. Nilesh Kumar Agarwal was honoured for his contribution as an outstanding author this year. Of the honour, He said "to be included in the distinguished and diversely talented company of the other Companions of Honour, especially as a writer, is a particular privilege."

CHAPTER ONE

It can be easy to get caught up in the details of a project and forget what got you started in the first place. It's important to remember that the beginning is always the hardest part. If you start off on the right foot, chances are you'll have a much easier time completing the rest of the project. Be prepared for obstacles, and don't be afraid to ask for help when you need it.

Starting a new project or task can always be challenging and there is often a feeling of resistance before getting started. It's important to remember that the beginning is usually the toughest part and that it gets easier as you continue. Taking small steps and breaking large tasks into smaller ones can help make the process more manageable. Additionally, setting achievable goals and making a plan of action will help to keep you on track. By recognizing that many projects start slowly, you can stay motivated while starting something new.

Starting something new can always be challenging. Whether it is a project, a business, or a new relationship, the beginning stages are often the most difficult for many people. It can be hard to know where to start and how to move forward. However, it's important to remember that every journey begins with a single step. With determination and perseverance, it is possible to overcome any challenge and make progress toward your goals. By staying focused on the end goal and taking one step at a time, you can push through any obstacle in your path.

There are countless people who have helped you along the way, whether they were directly involved in your project or not. It's important to recognize and be grateful for everyone who has helped you, whether it was giving you advice, lending a hand when you needed it, or simply motivating

you. Taking the time to reflect on these moments will help you to remember all of the people who have helped make your dreams a reality.

The saying goes that circumstances don't make the man, they only reveal him to himself. And while this may be true in some cases, it can also be misleading. For example, if you're struggling with a tough situation, it doesn't mean that you're not capable of greatness. In fact, you may just need to take a step back and assess the situation more carefully. This will help you to see yourself in a new light and achieve your goals. So be strong, even when things seem impossible.

When Tim Ferriss was a business undergraduate, his professor gave him a C- in his class and said that his business idea—starting and running an e-commerce store based out of his dorm room—would "never work." That idea was FedEx.

Despite the discouraging feedback, Ferriss persevered and founded one of the world's leading delivery services. In fact, FedEx is now worth an estimated $54 billion. If it can work for an established company like FedEx, there's no reason your business idea can't be successful, too.

To create a content brief that will help your project stand out from the crowd, make sure to include:
-An overview of the project

-A target

The founder of Robinhood, a no-fee stock trading app, was initially rejected by 75 venture capitalists. Now their startup is worth $7.6 billion.

Robinhood was founded in 2011 by Baiju Bhatt, who was initially rejected by 75 venture capitalists. The company has since raised over $1 billion in funding, making it one of the most successful startups in the United States. Thanks to its low fees and user-friendly interface, Robinhood has become a popular choice for stock traders.

When you make the decision to get serious about your life and your goals, you may lose some friends along the way. This is natural, as most people are comfortable with a somewhat casual relationship with their goals. However, when you start taking your career and life seriously, you may find that those friends who were once close become less interested in what you're doing.

Understanding this can help you to cope with the change. If you're willing to let go of some friendships, it may be worth it to pursue the things that are important to you. And if those friends don't want to change with you, that's okay too - there are plenty of other people out there who will support your dreams and aspirations.

There is a growing trend among billionaires not to have a college degree. According to Forbes, 80% of billionaires don't have a college degree. This is a stark contrast to the population as a whole, where nearly two-thirds of adults hold at least one degree. What factors may be contributing to this trend? It's possible that the rise of technology has caused some people to lose their jobs or find new opportunities without having to attend college. Additionally, there may be more opportunities available to those who are able to self-educate and don't need a traditional academic setting. There are also many billionaire entrepreneurs who have successful businesses without having a college degree.

You might be tempted to do this when you first meet someone, but it's never a good idea. You never know what a person is like inside, and you definitely don't want to start off on the wrong foot with them. Plus, if you judge someone by their appearance, you're likely to make negative assumptions about them. Keep in mind that people are more than just their looks.

If you're committed to your vision, you'll need to be willing to carry it out in a way that only you will see. Not everyone else will share in your vision, and that's okay. What matters is that you're working towards something that is important to you. Even if no one else sees it, that's what makes your journey special.

As parents, we often find ourselves giving our children a lot of advice. We tell them to brush their teeth, to eat their vegetables, to do their homework, and to clean their rooms. And while it's important to give our children this advice, it's even more important to lead by example.

If we want our children to brush their teeth, we need to brush our teeth. If we want our children to eat their vegetables, we need to eat our vegetables. If we want our children to do their homework, we need to do our homework. And if we want our children to clean their rooms, we need to clean our rooms.

In short, children will follow our example more than our advice. So, if we want our children to be happy and successful, we need to lead by example.

You learn nothing from life if you think you're right all the time. You learn from your mistakes, from your successes, and from the people around you. Life is a never-ending learning experience, and if you're not open to learning, you're not going to get very far. There's no shame in admitting that you don't know everything; in fact, it's one of the smartest things you can do. Be humble, be teachable, and always be learning.

Your terrible job is the dream of every unemployed. Your house is the dream of every homeless. Your smile is the dream of the depressed. Your health is the dream of the sick. Your love is the dream of the loveless. Your life is the dream of the dying.

Your health is the dream of the ill. Your lifestyle is the dream of somebody else. Don't let a difficult time make you forget your blessings. You are healthy and have the ability to live your life the way you want to. There are people who are sick and would love to have your lifestyle. During tough times, it is easy to forget the blessings we have. Try to remember the good things in your life and be thankful for them.

Everyone has negative thoughts, even positive people. The difference is that positive people don't let their negative thoughts take over and destroy them. They know that they

can't be happy all the time, but they also know that they can't let their negative thoughts take control. They focus on the positive and let the negative thoughts go.

There's no denying that everyone could use a little extra money. Whether you want to go on a luxurious vacation, save up for a down payment on a house, or simply have a cushion in your savings account, making more money is always a good idea.

There are a lot of ways to make extra money, from picking up a part-time job to investing in stocks or real estate. But if you're looking for a simple way to make more money, here are a few ideas:

1. Get a side hustle.

If you have a full-time job, you can always pick up a side hustle to make some extra cash. Whether you're driving for Uber, selling products on Etsy, or doing freelance work, there are plenty of ways to make money on the side.

2. Invest in yourself.

One of the best ways to make more money is to invest in yourself. Whether you're taking courses to learn new skills or investing in your own business, investing in yourself is a great way to make more money in the long run.

3. Save your money.

While it may seem counterintuitive, saving your money is a great way to make more money. If you're able to put away even a small amount each month, you'll be surprised at how quickly your savings will grow. And, if you're able to save up enough money, you can invest it and make even more money.

4. Make money from your hobbies.

If you have a hobby that you're passionate about, you can

actually make money from it. Whether you're a photographer, a musician, or a crafter, there are plenty of ways to turn your hobby into a money-making venture.

5. Get a higher-paying job.

If you're looking to make more money, one of the best things you can do is get a higher-paying job. While it may take some time and effort to land a higher-paying job, it will be worth it in the end.

Making more money is always a good idea, and there are a lot of ways to do it. Whether you're picking up a side hustle, investing in yourself, or getting a higher-paying job, there are plenty of ways to make more money. So, what are you waiting for? Start making more money today!

Some people think $60000 a year is great money. Some people think $60000 a month is a bad month. Surround yourself with those on the same mission as you and let their success inspire you. You'll get there. $60000 a year is a good salary in most places, but it's not an amazing salary. It's a comfortable salary that allows you to live a good life, but it's not going to make you rich.

The strongest among all factors for success is self-esteem. You don't need to convince others except yourself. You don't need the validation of others to feel good about yourself or your accomplishments. When you have self-esteem, you

believe in yourself and your abilities. You know that you are capable of achieving your goals. You don't let the opinion of others hold you back. You are confident in your own skin and you don't compare yourself to others. You accept yourself for who you are and you are comfortable in your own skin. When you have self-esteem, you are more likely to take risks and put yourself out there. You are more likely to pursue your dreams and goals. You are more likely to be successful in whatever you do because you believe in yourself.

Your life right now is a result of what you did a year ago. Your life a year from now will be a result of what you do right now. Act accordingly.

A year is a long time. It's enough time to make a significant change in your life if you're not happy with where you are. It's also enough time for things to stay exactly the same if you don't make any changes.

The choices you make today will determine what your life looks like a year from now. If you want to be in a different place, mentally, emotionally, or physically, you have to take action now.

You can't wait for things to happen. You have to make them happen. And it all starts with the decisions you make today. So choose wisely. Choose what will lead you to the life you want a year from now.

Whenever you want to buy something wait. Give yourself 7 days to decide before you purchase most often, you won't feel you need it anymore. This simple rule has saved me a lot of money over the years. If you can wait a week before buying something, you'll often find that you don't need or want it as much as you first thought. This is especially true for impulse purchases. If you can wait a week and still really want the item, then go ahead and buy it. But more often than not, you'll find that you don't need it after all.

Opinions are like cages, they can confine us and prevent us from truly living. Other people's opinions of us should never be allowed to dictate how we live our lives. We should always listen to our own inner voice and follow our own heart. When we do this, we are living our life authentically and in a way that is true to ourselves. This is the only way to truly be happy and fulfilled.

People who defend your name when you are not around are the most loyal friends you could ever get. These are the friends who will go to bat for you no matter what, and they will always have your back. These friends are worth their weight in gold, and you should cherish them.

Sometimes you think people are stopping you from getting to the top and forget it's your mouth. Stop negative self-talk. You are the only one who can hold yourself back. No one else has that power. So, the next time you find yourself thinking, "I can't do this," "This is too hard," or "I'm not good enough," stop and remind yourself that you are in control. You are the only one who can decide whether or not you succeed. Choose to believe in yourself and watch your life change for the better.

One negative word can ruin your entire life. So, be strong and respond less to negativity. People will always find something negative to say no matter who you are or what you do. It's important not to let the negative words of others get to you. You are in control of your own life and you should live it the way you want to. Don't let anyone else bring you down with their negative words.

Be careful, not everyone is a real friend. You might think you have a lot of friends, but how many of them are actually real friends? A real friend is someone who is there for you when you need them, not just when it's convenient for them. They're someone you can rely on, no matter what. They're also someone who accepts you for who you are, not who they want you to be. So be careful who you call your friend, because not everyone is worthy of that title.

If you want people to believe in your ideas, you have to believe in them first. Unfortunately, this is something that many people struggle with. We often allow doubts and negative thoughts to take over our minds, and before we know it, we've given up on our dreams. The truth is, it's okay to have doubts. In fact, they can be a sign that you're on the right track. But don't let them stop you from reaching your goals.

You wouldn't let just anyone live in your house. So why would you let anyone live rent-free in your head? If someone is an asshole, they don't get to live in your head and take up valuable space that could be used for so many other things. There are plenty of other people in the world who are worth your time and energy, so don't waste it on someone who isn't.

It's easy to make grandiose statements about what you're going to do. It's much harder to actually do it. And even harder still to keep doing it. But that's the only way to really get people's attention and respect. So don't just tell people what you're going to do, do it and shock them. And after shocking them, stay silent. Move onto your next project. Keep shocking.

When it comes to starting over, be prepared for disappointment. After all, you have been through the experience before and now you are expecting things to go differently. You are wrong. This time, you are starting from experience. When you start from experience, you have something to build off of. You have something to work with. You don't have to start from scratch every time because that is how you lose momentum and fail. But, don't be afraid to start over again because that is how you succeed.

When you're creating content, it's important to remember that you don't have to be like everyone else. In fact, it might be better if you stand out from the crowd. This will help you attract more attention to your content and make it more valuable to your audience. However, it's important to remember not to go too far overboard. If you become too different than your competitors, people may not be able to

relate to your work. Instead, try to create content that is unique and useful for your audience.

Working for someone else and not pursuing your own goals can be an easy trap to fall into. It's comfortable and safe, but not always the most fulfilling or rewarding. It's important to remember that you have your own dreams and ambitions, and you should never forget that. In this blog post, we'll be exploring why it's important to make time for yourself after work hours to work on your own goals and passions. We'll also look at how making this a priority can help you achieve success both in your professional and personal life.

It's no secret that succeeding in any venture requires dedication, hard work and a strong will to overcome challenges and obstacles. However, many people give up before they have a chance to truly reap the rewards of their efforts. According to statistics, It's true that 97% of people who quit too soon are employed by the 3% that preserved and didn't give up on their dreams. This statistic is a testament to the power of perseverance. Even when things seem bleak, it's important to remain focused on your goals and keep pushing forward despite any obstacles or hardships you may face. With determination, dedication, and hard work, you can make your dreams come true. Believe in yourself and never give up!

Achieving success is a journey that takes time and hard work, but many people still think they can achieve their dreams overnight. Whether it's in business, education, or personal relationships, the idea of instant gratification without putting in the work has become more popular than ever. Unfortunately, this mindset often leads to disappointment and frustration when things don't happen as quickly as expected. It is a common misconception that success comes easily and without hard work. Many people think that they can simply become successful overnight, without putting in the effort and dedication that it takes to actually achieve success. Unfortunately, this is not the case. Success requires dedication and hard work; it is a long-term goal that cannot be achieved by taking shortcuts or looking for quick fixes. If you want to be successful, you must be willing to put in the time and effort necessary to make your dreams come true.

With the pandemic still looming over the world, many of us may feel like we are stuck in limbo, struggling to adjust to our unfamiliar new normal. On top of the restrictions and changes that we have all had to make, it can be easy to let our frustrations get the best of us and start complaining about how little freedom we currently have. But before you do that, it's important to remember that not everyone has the privilege of a safe place to call home. Instead of complaining about being stuck at home, take a moment to reflect on those who are at risk of homelessness or living without access to basic necessities.

For many of us, our parents are the most important people in our lives. We strive to make them proud and give back all that they have given us throughout the years. But for some, their biggest dream is to be able to one day provide for their parents and give them the rest they deserve. My biggest dream is to be able to provide my father with the comfort and security that he deserves. I remember growing up, my dad worked hard to provide for our family and put in long hours to make sure we had what we needed. Now that I am older, I want nothing more than to be able to take over and give him the rest he needs and deserves. Knowing that I can provide for my family and make sure they have a comfortable and secure life is a dream come true. No words could express how much joy it would bring me to be able to turn around and tell

my dad, "Now you can rest easy; I'm here now".

We often find ourselves going through difficult situations in life that we wouldn't necessarily choose for ourselves. However, in these moments it is important to remember that everything we are going through is preparing us for what we asked for. Even if we don't understand it at the time, the challenges and storms of life are helping to shape us into who we need to be in order to achieve our goals. So, even when times are hard and you don't understand why certain things are happening, remember that everything you are going through is preparing you for what you asked for.

A wise person knows that there is something to be learned from every individual, no matter their background or experience. While this may sound like a cliché, it is an incredibly important truth that allows us to grow and expand our knowledge and understanding. By keeping an open mind and listening attentively to the views of others, we can gain valuable insights into different perspectives that can help us not only in our personal lives but also in our professional ones. Taking the time to learn from those around us will make us wiser and more capable individuals.

It is often said that "you will never make it if you care what others think." This phrase speaks to the importance of having a strong sense of self-confidence and trust in yourself and your decisions. When you are too concerned with the opinions of others, you can quickly become lost in indecision or find yourself unable to take action because of fear of failure or criticism. To truly succeed, you must be willing to take risks and trust your own judgement above all else. Being aware of what other people think is important, but at the end of the day, the only opinion that matters is your own.

If you want to make it in life, you need to focus on your own goals and dreams, and not worry about what other people may think. Too often, we let the opinions of others dictate our decisions and prevent us from taking risks that could be beneficial for our future. It is important to remember that the only person who can determine your success or failure is you, and no one else's opinion should matter more than your own. By taking ownership of your dreams and believing in yourself, you can turn any goal into a reality.

Those who don't clap when you win may be the people who are most honest with you. They can give you an unbiased, non-sugarcoated evaluation of your work that can help you improve and become better in the long run. It is important not to take their criticism personally, but rather to use it as an opportunity to reflect on how you can do better in the future. By taking this approach, you can ultimately use their

feedback to grow and become a more successful version of yourself.

When you have achieved something significant, it is natural to expect congratulations and applause from those around you. However, it is equally important to pay close attention to those who do not show encouragement or approval. Those who are envious or jealous may make themselves known by withholding praise, and their behavior should be taken as a sign that they are not true friends or allies. By paying attention to these people, you can understand where your relationships truly stand and act accordingly.

Patience is an important virtue that involves the ability to remain calm and composed in challenging situations. It is when you are supposed to get angry or frustrated but instead choose to take a step back and look for understanding. Patience allows us to take a breath and observe the situation, rather than immediately reacting in anger or frustration. This can help us to better understand why a particular event or situation has occurred, and how we can respond in an effective way. Ultimately, patience gives us the clarity and perspective that we need to make thoughtful decisions and stay calm in difficult situations.

Patience is a virtue that can be hard to practice in the face of adversity. It is easy to become frustrated and angry when things don't go as planned, but having patience allows us to take a step back and assess the situation. Rather than letting our emotions take over, patience allows us to choose understanding over anger. Through patience, we are able to think more clearly and rationally, giving us the opportunity to find solutions rather than creating more problems. Patience is an invaluable tool that can help make difficult situations more manageable and lead to outcomes that are more favorable for all involved.

Change is hard, but it doesn't have to be negative. Growing and learning in life can come with challenges that make things harder, but they can also bring growth and rewards. If your life has just become harder, congratulations! You've just leveled up. This means you are now on a journey of growth and development that should bring new knowledge and skills. As you face these changes, remember to celebrate the small victories along the way and don't be afraid to ask for help if you need it. Change is inevitable, embrace it and make the best of the opportunities it brings.

Life can be difficult at times and often throws us curveballs that make it more challenging. However, when we face those challenges head-on and come out the other side with a better understanding of ourselves and our capabilities, we should celebrate. Every time life gets harder, we should view it as an opportunity to level up and become stronger. The journey may be hard but the reward is worth it in the end. So if your life just got harder, congratulations – you just leveled up!

For many, the pursuit of success often comes at the cost of partying, socializing, and leisure activities. But for those who are serious about their goals and willing to take on the hard work and dedication it takes to reach them, there is a unique group that stands out from the rest. This group is known as the 1% club, and it includes those who are determined to make their dreams come true regardless of the sacrifices they must make along the way. By dedicating themselves to their goals and taking ownership of their own success, these individuals have become part of an exclusive group that is focused on achieving their ambitions.

If you're seeking success, a party might not be the first thing on your list. But when you commit to reaching your goals despite the allure of other activities, you join the exclusive 1% club. The members of this club are laser-focused on not only setting their targets but also meeting them in a timely manner. These individuals prioritize their aspirations over anything else and make it a point to stay motivated and disciplined in order to achieve their objectives. With dedication and hard work, they have managed to accomplish remarkable feats and are continuing to strive for even bigger accomplishments.

This is a wise adage that can be applied to many areas of life. It is especially true in terms of our choices and actions; we should be mindful of the potential consequences of our decisions. We should think before we act, as once we have dug ourselves into a hole, it may become impossible to get out. Even if we can manage it, the process of extrication will be difficult and time consuming. Therefore, it is better to exercise caution and restraint in order to avoid any

scenarios where the challenges become insurmountable.

The old adage "don't dig a hole so deep that even you can't get out of it" is an excellent reminder to be mindful of the decisions we make and the consequences they have. It's easy to get carried away and make risky choices, but it's important to take a step back and remember that sometimes the best option is not always the most exciting one. By being mindful of our actions, we can ensure that we don't find ourselves in a situation where we cannot extricate ourselves. So before making any important decisions, it pays to consider all of the possible outcomes — good and bad — so that you can make an informed choice.

We are all faced with difficult and unpredictable situations in our lives, but we cannot control the world around us. We can, however, choose how we respond to these events. Choosing to stay positive and focus on the things we can control allows us to maintain a sense of hope and optimism even in the most trying of times. It also helps to remind ourselves that our reactions are something within our power and that no matter what is happening in the world, we can still choose to stay hopeful, resilient, and determined.

It is easy to get overwhelmed by all the chaos happening in the world both on a global and personal level. During these times, it can be hard to remain focused and stay positive. However, it is important to remember that while we can't control what happens in the world, we do have some say in how we react to it. It is important to choose positivity and focus on what we can do rather than dwelling on what is out of our control. When faced with any situation, no matter how difficult or overwhelming, take a moment to pause and reflect on how you want to respond before taking action. By making conscious decisions about how you react during difficult times, you will ultimately be able to stay strong and resilient in the face.

Our abilities are essential in helping us achieve our goals, but it is ultimately our choices that dictate who we are and the life we live. We can choose to use our skills and talents for positive or negative ends, and no one can fully predict which choice we will make. Our choices reveal our character, goals, and values more than any of our inherent abilities. By making wise choices and staying true to ourselves, we can ensure that our life paths reflect what truly matters to us.

It is often said that it is not our abilities that show what we truly are, but rather our choices. The choices we make can reveal a great deal about who we are and what we stand for. By carefully considering our options and making decisions based on our values, we can demonstrate to the world the type of person we are. Our actions, then, become a reflection of ourselves and the values we hold dear. We must remember that, ultimately, it is not our abilities that determine who we are but the choices we make in life.

Training your mind to be calm in every situation is an essential part of self-care and mental wellness. Start by practicing mindfulness meditation, which can help you become aware of and accept your thoughts, feelings, and bodily sensations without judgement. You can also practice deep breathing techniques to slow down your heart rate and bring awareness to the present moment. Finally, try setting aside time each day for positive affirmations or visualizations, which can help you stay grounded in the present moment and cultivate a sense of inner peace. With consistent practice, you can train your mind to be calm even when faced with challenging situations.

Training your mind to stay calm in any situation can be a difficult task. It requires taking the time to practice mindfulness and meditation in order to become aware of your thoughts and emotions. When faced with a situation that stirs up feelings of stress or anxiety, take a few moments to breathe deeply and observe what is happening around you. This will help you to remain grounded in the present moment and take control of your thoughts. Additionally, engaging in activities such as yoga or journaling can also help to relax the body and mind, enabling you to maintain composure even in difficult situations. By taking the time to train your mind, you will be better equipped to stay calm no matter what life throws at you.

Unfortunately, it is sometimes the case that some people will never support you because they are afraid of what you might become. It could be that they are intimidated by your ambition and potential, or perhaps they are just threatened by the idea of change. Whatever the reason, such people will

always remain as a hurdle in your path to success. The best way to navigate these types of relationships is to focus on yourself and continue along your own path, without giving too much attention to those who don't see the same vision you have for yourself. With time, they may come around and recognize your talents, or they may remain in their own secure bubble with their own fears. Either way, it is important to not let them hold you back from reaching your goals

It is inevitable that some people will not support your journey and goals, no matter how hard you work. Unfortunately, this lack of support can often be rooted in fear. People fear change and the unknown, so when you are trying to create something new or reach your goals, some people may choose to support you from afar – or not at all. This can be difficult to accept, but it is important to remember that these reactions have nothing to do with you; instead they are based on the other person's own fears and insecurities. Rather than getting bogged down in negativity, stay focused on your goals and find the people who will help make those dreams a reality.

Overthinking is a habit of analyzing every detail of a situation until it becomes distorted. This can cause people to become overwhelmed with worry, fear, or doubt that may not even be based in reality. In many cases, overthinking can lead to the creation of problems that would not have existed if the situation had not been overanalyzed. Learning how to recognize when one is overthinking and taking steps to address the issue can help to reduce stress and create a healthier outlook on life.

Overthinking is a habit of focusing too much on a particular problem or situation, often to the point of creating problems that may not even exist. It can lead to increased stress and anxiety, as well as a lack of progress due to getting stuck in an unhelpful thought spiral. The key to overcoming overthinking is recognizing it when it happens and consciously redirecting your thoughts. Taking a mindful approach by focusing on the present moment and accepting reality as it is can help to break the cycle of overthinking and move forward more effectively.

If you are fortunate enough to be born in this moment of history, you have access to numerous resources and tools that can help you lead a fulfilling life. From the internet, to smartphones, to social media, technology has enabled us to access knowledge and opportunities that were previously unimaginable. In addition, it has made it easier than ever for us to connect with people around the world and share our passions and interests. With these tools at your disposal, you have an unprecedented ability to create a life of meaning and purpose.

If you were lucky enough to be born in this moment of history, you have access to countless opportunities that weren't available to previous generations. With the power of technology, you can connect with people around the world, learn new skills, and pursue your dreams. You have unlimited potential - so why not take advantage of it? Whether you are looking for a new career path or just want to expand your knowledge base, there are countless ways to make use of the resources available today. Take advantage of all that is available to you and make something amazing happen.

A 401k plan is a retirement savings plan offered by many employers to their employees. It allows employees to save money for retirement on a tax-deferred basis, meaning the contributions and any earnings on these investments are not taxed until withdrawn. Employers may often match employee contributions up to a certain percentage, making it an attractive option for those looking to save for the long term. The amount an employee can contribute to the plan annually is capped by the IRS, but this limit typically increases each year.

A 401k plan is an employer-sponsored retirement savings plan that allows employees to save for their future. It is a long-term, slow investment plan; typically, employers will match a portion of the employee's contributions. Funds in a 401k are generally invested in stocks, bonds, mutual funds, exchange-traded funds (ETFs), and other investment options. Contributions made to the 401k are tax-advantaged and can be withdrawn when the employee reaches retirement age, or in certain other situations. The 401k plan is a great way for employees to build a secure retirement fund while also receiving an employer match on their contributions.

It's a simple, yet profound truth: the more we focus on ourselves and our own growth, the more we will grow. Conversely, when we focus on all of the negative things in our lives - or 'shit' - those things will also grow. In order to truly experience personal growth, it is essential to put our energy into positive activities that cultivate physical, emotional, and spiritual health. This could include working out, engaging in creative hobbies, taking up yoga or mindfulness practices, and creating healthy relationships with those around us. By shifting our focus away from the negative aspects of life and towards what we can actively do to improve ourselves, we open up a world of opportunity for change.

Moving in silence is an important lesson to remember when navigating through life. It teaches us to be attentive and aware of our surroundings, to think before we act and speak, and to understand the power of knowledge and information. By moving in silence, we give ourselves the opportunity to observe, learn, and strategize a plan of action for when the time comes for us to make our move. We can then speak up with confidence and clarity when it's time to say checkmate. Moving in silence is not only beneficial for our own personal growth - it also shows respect towards those around us. When we listen more than we talk, we demonstrate humility and show that we value other people's opinions as much as our own. Ultimately, moving in

Moving in silence is a valuable lesson for anyone, no matter what their profession or field of work. It means that you stay focused and keep your attention to the task at hand instead of getting distracted by gossip and negativity. Additionally, it can also mean staying away from talking about your successes until you reach the point where you can truly say "checkmate" - when you have achieved a successful outcome and can proudly show off your hard work. By keeping quiet until then, you create an air of mystery around yourself and make sure that people take notice when you do eventually "checkmate".

There are two simple rules of success: never reveal everything you know, and never stop learning. Keeping your knowledge to yourself allows you to stay ahead of the competition, while at the same time remaining open to new ideas and opportunities for growth. By embracing a curious mindset and striving for continual learning, you can ensure that your knowledge is always up to date and relevant. Ultimately, these two rules will help you to stay competitive and successful in whatever field you pursue.

Whenever you feel discouraged about your business, it can be helpful to remember that even some of the most successful companies have had their ups and downs. Coca-Cola is a prime example of this. In the late 1800s, Coca-Cola was struggling to stay afloat. At one point, they only had one product—a syrup used to make soda—and sales were declining. However, they persevered and went on to become

one of the most successful companies in the world. This is an inspiring reminder that no matter how tough things seem, it's possible to turn things around with hard work and dedication.

Maturity is an important skill to have, especially when it comes to dealing with people and situations that may be harmful or threatening. Learning to walk away from unhealthy relationships and situations is a sign of emotional intelligence and strength. This doesn't mean giving up on the person or situation, but rather knowing when it's time to take a step back in order to protect yourself from further harm. It takes courage and wisdom to make this decision, but it can often be the best course of action for your own mental health and wellbeing.

Leadership is a trait that all successful people share, regardless of the industry they are in or the field they are working in. Leaders have an ability to take charge and guide people towards a common goal. They are also able to motivate and inspire others to excel at whatever task lies ahead. Leaders possess a unique vision that allows them to stay focused on the big picture and make decisions that will benefit everyone involved. Leadership also involves being able to think strategically, manage resources wisely, and build strong relationships with team members. Ultimately,

successful leaders know how to bring out the best in those around them and help them reach their full potential.

It's true, a million-dollar will never come from your comfort zone. To achieve success and growth, you need to step outside that box and take risks. This can be daunting at first, but once you face the fear of the unknown and put yourself in uncomfortable situations, you will find that there is great potential waiting for you. By pushing yourself to try new things and embrace challenges, you are paving the way for a more successful future. So remember, a million-dollar will never come from your comfort zone!

Your mentality and the people you choose to surround yourself with can have a huge impact on your success. Make sure that you have a positive mentality, as this will help to shape your goals and make it easier to stay motivated. Additionally, seek out mentors who have experience in the areas where you want to succeed. Surrounding yourself with successful people can help to inspire and motivate you, making it easier to reach your goals. At the end of the day, success is determined by your mindset and the mentors that you choose. Choose them wisely!

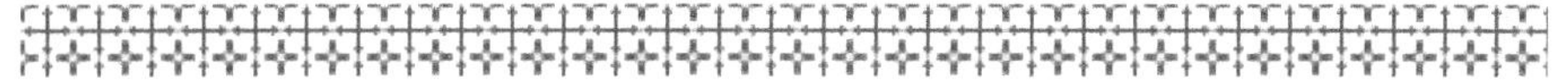

No matter how hard the world tries to hold you back, it is important to never give up. Life can be difficult and filled with obstacles that can seem insurmountable. However, by continuing to push forward and take action, no matter how small the steps may be, you can make progress towards your goals. It is essential to remember that success doesn't happen overnight and there will be setbacks along the way. But by staying focused and motivated, you can achieve anything you set your mind to. So no matter how hard life tries to keep you down, always keep striving for greatness!

Kobe Bryant was widely known for his insane work ethic and dedication to his craft. According to a team USA trainer, Kobe once worked out for 10 hours straight without any breaks or rest. He would take only short breaks every hour or two to stretch and eat some food, but he never stopped working until he was finished. This commitment to hard work and dedication is what helped him become one of the greatest basketball players of all time.

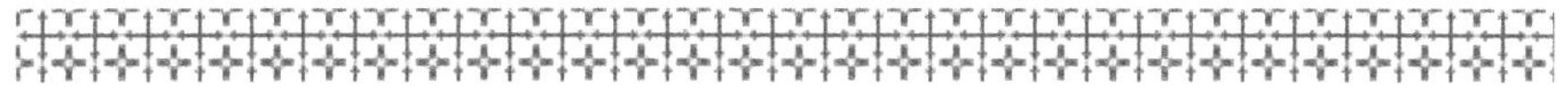

Many people rely on their salary as their only source of income, but this can be extremely risky. If something unexpected happens and you are unable to work, you may find yourself one step away from poverty. This means that having a reliable stream of income is essential for financial security. To ensure financial stability, it is important to have multiple sources of income such as investments, side hustles, or passive income streams. These additional sources will help you to have a cushion in case of an emergency and provide long-term security.

We all have the same 24 hours in a day. While this amount of time may feel limiting, the truth is that it is up to us to make the most of it and be productive. The only difference between successful people and those who are not is how they choose to spend their time. By focusing on tasks that are important and meaningful, we can make the most of our limited time and achieve our goals. Additionally, by taking regular breaks to relax, we can ensure that we stay energized and motivated throughout the day. No matter how busy our lives may be, there is always an opportunity to make something valuable out of our 24 hours each day."

Beauty is big business, reaching an estimated global market of $532 billion in 2018. However, while the industry may be lucrative, it's important to recognize that buying beauty

products won't make you "pretty" or give you self-confidence. That's something that comes from within. In contrast, investing in education can have a lasting and positive impact on both your career prospects and sense of self-worth. Education is estimated to be a $13 trillion industry worldwide, and has been linked to higher incomes and better quality of life for individuals. So, if you're looking to use your money wisely and gain something meaningful from it, investing in your education rather than the beauty industry might be best way to go.

people can have an incredibly powerful impact on our lives. It helps us to explore our thoughts and ideas, stimulates creativity, encourages problem-solving, and builds connection. When we engage in thoughtful conversations with those around us who have a different perspective or life experiences, we can open ourselves up to understanding and growth. It gives us the opportunity to learn new things, challenge our beliefs and biases, and cultivate empathy. Deep conversations can offer priceless insight that is otherwise unavailable to us – making it an invaluable tool in both our professional and personal lives.

Bill Gates and Paul Allen were two college dropouts who had a shared vision to create something special. They started Microsoft in 1975, and the rest is history. Larry Page and

Sergey Brin also had a shared dream of creating something unique, leading them to launch Google in 1998. Both tech giants have had an enormous impact on the world, creating products and services that have changed the way we interact with technology. While their paths may have been different, both Bill Gates and Larry Page have demonstrated what can be achieved through sheer hard work and determination.

It is inspiring to look at what Jack Ma and his 8 friends were able to accomplish with the founding of Alibaba. Starting a business from the ground up is no easy feat, but with hard work and dedication, it can be done. Even if you don't have your own business dream in mind, there are countless ways to make use of the power of friendship. From starting a club or charity organization, to organizing a fundraiser or even just having dinner together, you can take advantage of your friendships to do something amazing. Take inspiration from Jack Ma and his 8 friends and see what you and your friends can accomplish!

We often look to the past as a source of guidance and understanding, but it is important to remember that our current lives are not defined by our past experiences. Instead, we should strive to use the lessons we have learned from our mistakes and successes in order to make better decisions in the future. It is easy to become bogged down by feelings of regret or guilt over past events, but this will only hinder our progress going forward. Everyone should be free to make their own choices and pursue their goals without being held back by the things that have happened in the past.

Making money is a skill that anyone can learn. It doesn't take a genius or an Ivy League degree to become financially successful. All it takes is good business acumen and the right mindset. The key to success lies in understanding the value of each dollar you make and then multiplying that value through smart investments and savvy business practices. Learning how to make a single dollar can be your first step towards making a million more. So, if you think you have what it takes, start investing today and see how far your money can take you.

It's important to remember that great things take time, and that success rarely happens overnight. Patience is a virtue, and it's necessary in order to keep going and stay motivated on the path towards achieving your goals. Additionally, it's important to never give up. It may feel like you aren't making progress, but even small steps can eventually lead to big results. With patience, dedication, and hard work, anything is possible.

We are living in an age where technology can be used to create amazing things and to make the world a better place. From electric cars to rockets, there is no limit to what you can build and create with the right tools and resources. Through using these new technologies, you can make a real difference in improving the environment and helping people get access to basic needs. Not only that, but you can also use your skills for positive change by creating educational materials, developing renewable energy sources, or even volunteering for a cause that is important to you. With the right mindset and dedication, you can truly make a difference and help shape our future for the better!

Achieving your dreams requires a certain amount of sacrifice and hard work. You need to be willing to give up some of your comfort, convenience, or time in order to make the necessary progress towards achieving your goals. If you're not willing to make these sacrifices, then it's very likely that your dream will never become a reality. It's important to recognize that some things are worth sacrificing for, and if you don't have the determination and ambition necessary to make these sacrifices, then you can't expect any kind of success in the future. Don't let fear stop you from taking risks and investing in yourself. Put in the hard work now and reap the rewards later.

It's often said that the key to success is doing what others won't. This means being willing to put in extra effort, be creative and think outside the box, and push yourself further than others are willing to go. By doing this, you create opportunities for yourself that most people don't have. You can develop skills and knowledge that set you apart from the ever-growing crowd of competitors. By investing in yourself like this, you can gain an edge over your peers, and have the chance to experience successes that they may never have. So when faced with a challenge, be willing to do what others don't so you can have what they can't.

Wake up early, stay up late – it can be tempting to think that these are the keys to success. However, it's not so much about getting up earlier or staying up later that makes the difference, but rather what you do with your time during those hours. Whatever your schedule is like, make sure that you're using your time in a productive manner, focusing on activities that will help you reach your goals and realize your ambitions. Whether it's reading books or taking an online course, make sure you're putting in the time and effort necessary to achieve success.

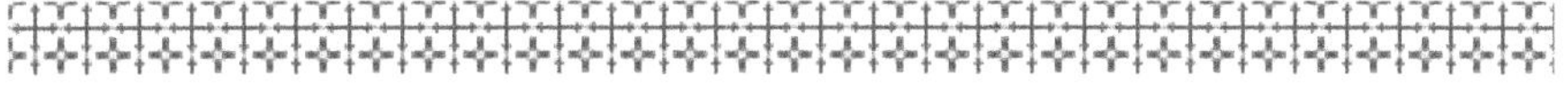

We all have days when we feel down and want to cry, but it's important to remember that no one else can know our innermost thoughts and feelings. Instead of giving in to tears, take a moment to remind yourself of the power of a smile. When you put on your best face and start smiling, people will naturally be drawn to you, and they may even become jealous of your positive attitude. A smile is an infectious emotion that can have a ripple effect, ultimately leading to more happiness for everyone around you.

The largest package delivery company in the world, FedEx, was founded by two teenagers with a simple idea. In 1971, Fred Smith and his friend Robert Spediacci had the ambitious goal of creating a delivery service that could move packages from Point A to Point B faster than any other company. Their company quickly grew from its humble beginnings to become one of the biggest companies in the industry. Over time, they revolutionized the way companies shipped packages and made it easier to transport goods around the world. Today, FedEx is one of the most successful companies in history and continues to be a leader in package delivery services.

It is important to remember that no one knows what's best for you better than you. No matter how negative someone may be, it is essential to keep in mind that their opinions

are not necessarily the only truth. Instead of listening to the negative opinions of others, focus on what makes you happy in everyday life and strive to achieve it. It could be anything from a new hobby or skill to a goal that you have been trying to reach for some time. By doing this, you will be able to stay motivated and work towards creating a fulfilling life for yourself despite any external negativity.

Luck is a term often used by those who are jealous of others' successes. When someone else has achieved something that they themselves could not, they may attempt to explain it away as luck. It is a way of minimizing the hard work, dedication, and ambition that went into that person's success. It can be used as a way to make oneself feel better about not having achieved the same thing. However, in reality, luck usually plays only a small part in one's success; hard work and determination are usually necessary for true success.

It's true that, when you drive in a Ferrari, no one will care about what degree you have. They will not be interested in where you went to school or how much money you make. Instead, they will be envious of the fact that you are driving such an iconic and luxurious car. Nonetheless, having an impressive degree can still open doors for you, as it often signals to employers that you are capable and hard-working.

In other words, your degree may help to get your foot in the door, but it won't necessarily guarantee success.

Treating others with respect is an invaluable life skill and one that costs nothing to practice. Respect involves treating others with dignity, courtesy, and understanding, while listening to their opinions and ideas without judgement. It also means valuing the unique qualities of each individual and recognizing their right to express themselves in a safe environment. Respect can go a long way in establishing meaningful relationships with those around us, both professionally and personally. Therefore, it's worth investing time and energy into developing this important skill – it costs nothing but pays off dividends in the end.

Reaching the top of any field can be a daunting challenge. It takes hard work, dedication and perseverance to achieve success in any endeavor. However, one key factor that is often overlooked is mindset. Thinking like a champion and believing that you are already at the top, even when you are far from it, can help propel you to reach heights you never thought possible. Studies have shown that those with a strong belief in their own abilities and talents have greater success than those who lack in confidence. By believing that you are already at the top, you create an inner drive to put in the effort to get there. By having this mindset, you will find

yourself taking the steps needed to reach your goals more quickly and easily.

Lamborghini is a luxury car brand that doesn't advertise through traditional television commercials. The company has found that their target market is already aware of their product and its prestige, so there's no need to advertise in a more traditional way. They understand that those who can afford their cars are likely to be well-informed on the brand and its offerings, making television advertising superfluous. Instead, Lamborghini focuses their marketing efforts on events and word of mouth, as well as digital content such as social media campaigns.

Everyone deserves respect, regardless of their profession. As a society, we should strive to recognize that everyone has the right to work and be respected for their efforts. This includes doctors, cleaners, and all other occupations. Everyone should be treated with dignity and respect, without any kind of judgement or mockery. We must remember that a job is a job, regardless of whether it is seen as prestigious or not. Everyone has the right to work and should be encouraged to do so without being demeaned for their decisions. By recognizing this fact, we can ensure that everyone is treated with the same level of respect, no matter what job they choose.

It is easy to get caught up in what other people think and allow their opinions to shape your decisions, but it is important to remember that the only opinion that matters is yours. Other people's opinions don't pay the bills and they don't make you happy. You have to be comfortable with who you are and what you want in order to make decisions that are best for you. At the end of the day, it is only your opinion that counts, so make sure you trust yourself above all else.

It is important to spend time with people who are working towards the same goals and ambitions as you are. Surrounding yourself with people who share similar values and interests can help you stay motivated and focused on

your own objectives. This is especially true when it comes to achieving success in the future. Hanging out with people from your past may bring comfort in the present, but if their goals do not align with yours, it can be difficult to move forward without feeling held back. Invest in relationships that will help you reach for your dreams and build a future filled with purpose.

In 2015, Beyoncé made headlines when she performed for Uber and instead of accepting the $6million offered, she requested equity in the company. This move proved to be a shrewd one, as her stake in Uber was worth an estimated $300 million when it went public in 2019. Beyoncé was not only able to make a large profit from her investment, but also help raise awareness of the ride-sharing giant. Her performance pushed the brand into the mainstream and helped secure its place as one of the most successful companies in the world.

It is an unfortunate but true reality that people will quit on you at times. No matter how successful you become, there will always be people who do not believe in your vision and quit when things get tough. However, you must never lose sight of your goals and continue to work hard every day. While it can be disheartening to have people quit on you, it is important to remember that only you have the power to

keep going no matter what. It is essential that you maintain a resilient attitude and never quit on yourself. With this mindset, even the toughest setbacks can be overcome and success can follow.

According to recent reports, 40% of Google's employees have not attended college. This statistic speaks to the company's commitment to diverse hiring and its recognition of skill sets beyond academic achievement. Although a college degree may be an advantage in certain situations, Google looks for candidates who possess qualities including leadership potential, problem-solving skills, creativity, and technical proficiency. These are the qualities that Google values most when making hiring decisions, regardless of the candidate's educational background.

Many people are familiar with the adage "grind in your 20's, build in your 30's, and chill in your 40's." This generally refers to the idea that young adults should take the opportunity to work hard and take risks while they are still young. In their 30's, this energy should be used to build on those successes and create stability in their lives. Finally, when they reach their 40's, they can relax and enjoy the fruits of their labor. By following this advice, it is possible for people of any age to have a successful life.

It can be tempting to tell others about your projects and ideas before they are complete, but it's important to remember that doing so can throw off the energy that is needed to finish them successfully. Keeping your ideas to yourself until you are sure you are ready for feedback or criticism can help ensure that the project stays focused and on track. It also prevents any negative energy from derailing your progress. Additionally, by keeping your plans a secret until you know they are finished, you will be able to surprise those around you with a finished product.

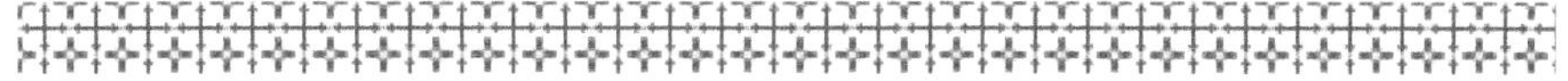

It is often said that losers make mistakes and then they make excuses, while winners make mistakes and then they make adjustments. This is an important distinction to remember when trying to create lasting success. When faced with a mistake, it is important to take the time to assess what went wrong and determine the best way forward. This could involve changing strategies, seeking advice from experts or even starting fresh. By objectively analyzing the situation and making the necessary adjustments, you can not only prevent further mistakes but also ensure lasting success in whatever endeavor you are pursuing.

Competition is an inherent part of many activities in life, from sports to business to academics. When faced with a competitive situation, it is easy to become overwhelmed and stressed out. However, the best way to respond to competition is not to take it too seriously and instead focus on having fun. By doing this, you can reduce stress levels and enjoy the process more. Taking competition too seriously can lead to burnout and frustration. Instead, by focusing on having a good time and enjoying the experience, you can stay motivated and energized while still achieving your goals.

Being an effective leader is about more than just being in front and leading the charge; it's about taking care of your team. Leaders should be focused not just on their own success, but on ensuring that their teams have the resources and support they need to be successful. This means having a clear vision and communicating it to everyone on the team, providing constructive feedback, and recognizing their hard work. A good leader knows that taking care of their team comes before personal gain and sets an example for how others should treat each other. Being a leader is not just about being in front, but rather creating a safe and supportive environment where everyone can thrive.

It is said that if you surround yourself with five confident people, you will be the sixth. This holds true because the energy and confidence of those around you can influence your own attitude. Being around confident people can make you believe in yourself more, which can open up a world of opportunities. Additionally, these people can provide valuable advice on different topics, such as career or relationships. Furthermore, confident people create an atmosphere of positivity, which can be contagious and help to keep your spirits up when times are tough. So if you want to boost your own confidence, seek out five confident people that you admire and hang around them!

Marketing and branding go hand in hand when it comes to creating an effective strategy for your business. Marketing is like asking someone out on a date - you're making your pitch, introducing yourself, and hoping they find you desirable. Branding, on the other hand, is the reason they say "yes". It can be thought of as the personality of your business - what makes you unique and different from other competitors. By establishing a strong brand identity that speaks to your target audience and communicates who you are as a business, you can make sure that your marketing efforts are successful.

Starting a business is an exciting moment, but it can also be overwhelming. As you begin to plan and execute your business venture, you quickly realize how much work is involved. From writing a business plan to finding financing to marketing the product or service, there are countless details that must be considered and addressed. It can be easy to feel overwhelmed with the enormity of the task at hand, but in doing so, it's important not to lose sight of why you started the business in the first place. It's essential to stay focused on your goals and remain optimistic about achieving success in order to ensure that your business will take off.

The practice of setting a fixed amount of time for each task and integrating the Pomodoro Technique into your workflow can be an effective way to stay focused and productive. The Pomodoro Technique involves setting a timer for 25 minutes and working on one task until the timer goes off. This method helps to break down large tasks into more manageable chunks, while also helping to keep you motivated by providing short breaks in between tasks. Additionally, this technique can help to eliminate procrastination by allowing you to focus on one task at a time without any distractions. By taking the time to plan out your day with timed intervals, you can maximize your productivity and efficiency.

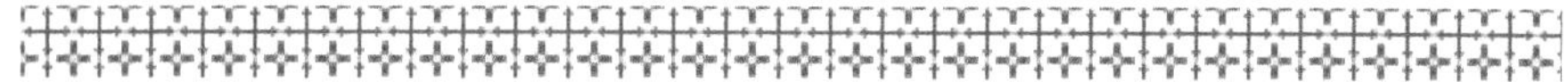

The weekend is a great time to take stock of your life and make progress on the things that you want to achieve. Instead of using the weekend to escape from the realities of your daily life, use it as an opportunity to build the life that you want. Take some time to plan out your goals for the upcoming week and create a strategy for how you will reach them. You can also use this time to do something enjoyable, such as going on a hike or taking a yoga class with friends. By investing in yourself on the weekend, you can set yourself up for success during the rest of the week.

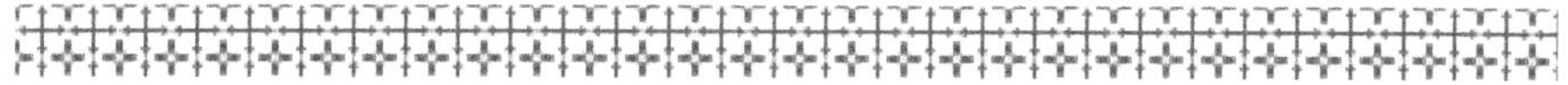

If you want to improve your life, you need to be willing to pay the "true cost" of doing so. This means spending time and money on things that may not be easy or fun, but are necessary if you want to reach your long-term goals.

Sometimes we put off making tough decisions because we think they will be too hard or expensive. But if you really want a better life, you must be willing to pay the "true cost" of getting there. This means being more than just successful; it means achieving something truly great. So be brave and give it everything you've got!

The old adage that money can't buy happiness is still widely accepted, but it is important to realize there are certain things that only money can buy. Money allows us to purchase luxuries like private jets and designer handbags, which are not available without financial means. While these items may bring some temporary joy or satisfaction, they do not equal true happiness. True happiness can only be found from relationships, experiences and meaningful accomplishments. Money certainly makes life easier in many ways, but it cannot replace genuine contentment and joy.

The proverb 'Money doesn't buy happiness' is a reminder to us all that material wealth is not a guaranteed path to contentment in life. It is true that having money can provide access to material comforts, but it cannot guarantee long-term satisfaction or joy. On the other hand, poverty buys nothing. Those who are poor often lack access to basic necessities such as food, shelter, healthcare and education. This can lead to feelings of hopelessness and despair which cannot be remedied by money. In short, both money and poverty can be sources of hardship and suffering if not managed responsibly.

Everyone has an excuse for why they can't do something. They might complain about lack of time, money, or resources. But these obstacles should never prevent you from reaching your goals and achieving success. Opportunities come and go, but if you don't take the chance to seize them when they arise then they will be gone forever. Excuses

will always be there for you, but opportunity won't. It's important to recognize the difference between excuses and real problems that stand in your way. By taking action and not letting excuses hold you back, you open yourself up to new possibilities and can make progress towards your dreams.

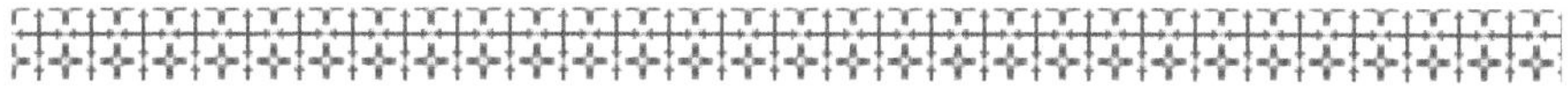

The quote "Never tell people your plans. Show them your results." is a reminder that actions speak louder than words. By keeping our ambitions and goals to ourselves, we can avoid being judged or criticized before we have even taken the first step towards achieving them. Instead, it is better to focus on delivering tangible results that demonstrate our commitment and drive in reaching our aspirations. By doing so, we can inspire others with our accomplishments and demonstrate that anything is possible with enough dedication and hard work.

Getting rich is indeed a game, but it's not one that you can win overnight. It requires knowledge of the markets, strategic decisions and an understanding of long-term trends in order to maximize your gains. Additionally, it requires patience and foresight to ensure that investments are made with the best possible outcome in mind. Understanding each of these components will help you

become a successful investor and increase your chances of achieving greater wealth.

The phrase "You get paid for your value, not your time" is often used to encourage people to focus more on providing valuable services and products, rather than simply trading their time for money. In other words, it is important to focus on delivering services or products of high quality that are beneficial to the customer or client. Remember that customers don't just pay for a service, they pay for the value they receive from it. So it is important to strive to provide as much value as possible in order to ensure you are properly compensated.

Becoming a millionaire is a dream for many, and there are two ways to make it happen. The first way is to find a problem and solve it – this can be done through developing a new product or service, creating an innovative solution, or creating an entirely new industry. The second way is to find an existing problem and capitalize on it – this could involve investing in stocks and real estate, leveraging existing businesses, or starting your own venture. No matter which route you choose, the key is to be creative and tenacious in order to reach your goal of becoming a millionaire.

The idea of what it means to live a successful life has changed over the years. No longer is having a nice car, a house, and a degree enough to signify success. Instead, showing off one's accomplishments in more creative ways has become the ultimate flex. For example, starting a business or taking an unconventional career path can be seen as signs of achievement. Demonstrating your knowledge and skills on social media is another way to flex your success. In this digital age, it's important to showcase yourself on platforms like Instagram and LinkedIn in order to show that you are well-rounded and successful.

In an ever-changing world, time freedom, location freedom, and financial freedom are becoming increasingly important. This means that having the ability to work from anywhere in the world and have the financial flexibility to pursue our passions is becoming a highly valued status. Furthermore, having good physical and mental health is becoming increasingly important as a measure of success. With advances in technology, it's never been easier to achieve these freedoms and take control of our lives. It's time to embrace this new shift in status and start working towards achieving our goals.

Taking risks is essential for personal and career growth. People who don't take risks will never achieve their full potential, as they will always be relying on someone else to

do the hard work and make the bold decisions. By taking calculated risks, you can move forward with confidence knowing that your risk has been carefully thought out and could lead to great rewards. However, it is important to remember that the only way to truly benefit from taking a risk is if you are willing to accept the consequences of failure. Taking risks gives us the opportunity to learn, grow and develop as individuals and professionals.

Trying and failing is often seen as a failure, but the truth is that it takes a great deal of courage and strength to try something new and difficult. While it can be disheartening to not succeed on the first attempt, it is essential to understand that taking risks and trying something new is an important part of growth. If you try something and fail, congratulations; most people never even take the step of attempting it in the first place. Whether it's starting a business, learning a new skill, or venturing into an unfamiliar territory, don't let the fear of failure stop you. Take the opportunity to congratulate yourself for having taken action and use your experience as an opportunity for further growth.

A bar of iron is a valuable resource that has different uses and corresponding value depending on what it is used for. The cost of a bar of iron is $5, but its worth increases when

made into horseshoes, as it increases to $12. If the same bar of iron is made into needles, its worth increases even more significantly and can be sold for much higher prices.

The same principle can be applied to ourselves. We all have a unique set of skills, abilities, and potential that we can use to make something of ourselves. By embracing our potential and striving to make the best use of our skills, we can create great things that have real value. As the old saying goes, "Your own value is determined also by what you are able to make of yourself." When we invest time and effort into turning ourselves into something more than we were before, it pays off in ways that cannot be quantified in monetary terms.

Walking alone can be a daunting task, but it doesn't have to be. When life throws us challenging situations, it is important to remember that we are never truly alone. We can always put our trust in ourselves, knowing that we are capable of persisting through any adversity. By walking with the assurance that we have the strength and character to overcome any obstacle, we can confront any situation with confidence and a positive attitude. In this way, walking alone can be an empowering experience that helps build our resilience and self-esteem.

This phrase is a reminder that we should never be afraid to dream big or think outside the box. When we hear criticism and even laughter from those around us, it can be easy to doubt our ideas and dreams. However, if our goals are not inspiring enough to provoke disbelief and even ridicule, then they are likely not ambitious enough. It's important to remember that challenging ourselves and striving for something greater is what leads to success and fulfills our potential. So don't let anyone bring you down - keep dreaming, keep striving, and don't be afraid of big goals!

It is often said that direction is more important than speed – and this is true in many aspects of life. Many people are going very fast, but they may be heading in the wrong direction. It is essential to have a clear idea of the destination, the goal, or the mission. Without a clear direction, even if one moves quickly, they may end up somewhere they hadn't intended. Taking time to think through the desired course of action can help ensure that one reaches their desired destination quickly and efficiently.

Don't be discouraged if you find yourself having to go it alone. It can often be a more fulfilling experience than going with company, as it gives you the opportunity to focus on yourself and your own goals. It also allows you to take time to enjoy the journey and learn more about yourself in the

process. Remember that no one else can walk your path for you, so make sure to embrace the opportunity of walking alone and make the most out of it. By doing so, you'll come out of it a stronger, wiser individual with an even greater appreciation for life's little journeys.

Posting your achievements and successes on social media can be a great way to show off your accomplishments. However, it can also have the opposite effect and make you appear boastful or arrogant. Instead, focus on posting entertaining content such as funny jokes or memes. This will make you seem more approachable and friendly, which may draw people to your page. Additionally, people are more likely to engage with humorous topics than serious ones, so it will help boost your engagement rate on social media. So remember, when it comes to social media posts – never post your achievements; instead focus on stupid stuff and jokes!

Posting stupid things online can be a surefire way to make people think you don't have much of a future ahead of you. People generally don't like it when others seem to be stuck in the past and unwilling to move forward, and this can be especially true when it comes to progress. By posting silly or outdated content, you risk giving off the impression that you are behind the times and not particularly open to new ideas. As such, it is best to avoid posting anything that could cause others to question your aptitude for progress.

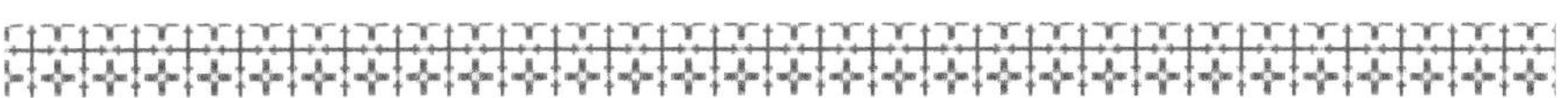

The phrase "if hard work made you rich, day laborers would be millionaires" is a popular adage that has been used for centuries. It speaks to the idea that success does not always come from hard work alone. Instead, it often requires a combination of hard work, luck, and access to resources. Day laborers are a perfect example of individuals who work extremely hard, but often lack access to the necessary resources to become wealthy or even comfortable. This phrase serves as an important reminder that everyone has their own unique set of circumstances and individual success should be celebrated rather than compared.

Everyone has dreams and aspirations. It all starts with a dream of what we want our lives to become. We can use those dreams as a starting point to build the lives we want. Dreams give us hope, help us stay motivated, and provide direction. They also remind us of our resilience and strength when faced with challenges. Turning dreams into reality takes hard work, but it is possible if we persevere. So never stop dreaming and take the steps needed to make them come true.

Waiting for tomorrow to make changes in our lives can be a detrimental habit. While it is important to plan for the future and make long-term goals, it is also important to take action today and start making progress towards those goals. Starting now means taking advantage of every opportunity that comes your way and utilizing the resources you already have. Taking small steps each day towards what you want to achieve will quickly add up in the long run and help you get closer to your dreams. Stop waiting for tomorrow and start now!

our decisions are a direct reflection of who you are and where you want to be. Every decision you make will have an impact on your future. Whether it is small or big, your decisions can make or break you. In order to be successful, it is important to make good decisions that reflect your values and goals. Taking the time to thoughtfully consider the consequences of each decision before making it can help you reach your goals and avoid pitfalls along the way. Being aware of how your choices shape your future will help ensure that you can look back with pride on the decisions that you have made.

Making the right decisions is essential for success, and this is especially true when starting a business. Ronald Wayne, the third co-founder of Apple, served as a prime example of this. Although he was integral to the beginnings of Apple, he eventually sold his shares for just $800 and left the company before it reached its full potential. This showed that even seemingly small decisions can have huge implications in the long run, and it's important to consider all possible *outcomes before making a final decision.*

Helping one person might not change the world in a major, sweeping way, but it could have an incredible impact on that person's life. Even small acts of kindness can make someone feel supported, appreciated and seen. From donating to a charity to buying someone a cup of coffee, even little gestures can be life-changing for the people we interact with on a daily basis. It's important to remember that everyone is fighting their own battles and those small acts of kindness can help bring some much-needed joy or relief into their life.

The proverb "Nobody cares about your story until you win, so win" is a reminder that success matters. People may be interested in hearing your story, but unless you are able to achieve something, it won't have any lasting impact. It is important to strive for excellence and to never give up in the face of adversity. If you work hard, stay focused, and remain positive, then you can ultimately reach your goals. This proverb encourages us to keep our eyes on the prize and make sure that we put in the effort necessary to succeed.

Thinking is an incredibly difficult process and requires a great deal of training and practice to become skilled at it. It is important to be well-versed in the basics of critical thinking, such as problem solving, decision making, and analyzing arguments. In addition to that, it is essential to understand the context of a problem in order to apply the right solutions. This means having a keen understanding of the subject matter and being able to identify patterns or trends that can lead one to the right answer. Finally, it is important to stay focused on a task and have an inquisitive mindset when working through difficult problems. With time, effort, and dedication you can hone your thinking skills and come up with creative solutions that will help you reach success. We all have different sides to our personality and we often argue with ourselves internally. To succeed in life, it is essential to be able to recognize those different sides of yourself and to use them productively. When faced with a challenge or difficult decision, you should try to let the two sides of yourself "have a war" in your head. This means that you should carefully weigh both sides of the issue, considering the pros and cons objectively before making a decision. By giving each side a chance to be heard, you can make sure that all angles are considered, helping you come up with an informed and well-rounded decision.

Books act as a bridge to a better life and the knowledge you acquire from them will have long-term effects. Reading has been shown to increase empathy, foster creativity, and improve communication and problem solving skills.

Furthermore, books act as a gateway for learning about different cultures and ideas, enabling people to gain a broader understanding of the world. By reading books, we can gain new perspectives and open our minds to new possibilities in life. Books are also valuable sources of information that can be used for research or simply learning more about a particular topic. In short, books serve as an essential tool for growth and self-development by providing us with knowledge that will be beneficial in the long run.

Working while others sleep, learning while they party, saving while they spend, and living your dreams: all of these are achievable goals that require a little bit of extra effort. Working hard during the day can help you to save more money and set aside funds for future investments. Learning new skills in your spare time can help you reach a higher level in your career. And living out your dreams will give you the motivation to keep going and strive for more. By following this mantra, you can take control of your life and make the most of each moment.

Everyone is capable of achieving something great, no matter their age. Unfortunately, society often tells us that young people don't have the same opportunities as older generations. However, even a baby can accomplish amazing things if they are given the right opportunity and support.

It's important to not let other people's opinions limit you or hold you back from achieving your goals. Believe in yourself and remember that age is just a number– you can do anything if you put your mind to it!

The phrase "a baby tiger is still a tiger" is often used to remind people that age does not define their capability or potential. No matter how young you are, you can still make a difference and do great things in the world. This message of empowerment holds true for all ages, from children to adults. It's never too early to start making a positive impact on the world, no matter what your age. With determination, hard work and perseverance, anyone can make a difference regardless of their age.

Starting something new can seem daunting, especially when working a 9-5 job. However, it is possible to make time for what matters most to you and find success. To get started, begin by setting aside a few hours each week focused on your dream project. Even if it's just an hour or two, this dedicated time can make all the difference in achieving your goal. Additionally, look for areas of your day-to-day life where you can become more efficient and free up extra time. By finding ways to work smarter and make the most out of every hour, you can carve out enough time to pursue your passions.

If you're working a typical 9-5 job, then chances are you have plenty of time that could be used more productively. It is easy to feel like all the time spent in the office is wasted, but with a bit of creativity and planning, you can use this time to make progress on your own personal and professional goals. Even small tasks like reading articles or blog posts, catching up on emails, or connecting with colleagues can help you stay productive and make the most of your day. By taking advantage of this wasted time and setting aside some dedicated time for yourself each day, you can start to make meaningful progress towards achieving your goals.

The saying "a little progress each day adds up to big results" is a powerful reminder of the importance of small steps. Making a bit of progress each day can have a significant impact when the progress is compounded over time. By taking consistent, even incremental actions each day, it is possible to turn small actions into much larger accomplishments. Whether that means achieving a personal goal or completing a task, by making steady progress each day, great achievements are within reach.

Everyone has experienced a challenging time in their life when it seemed like nothing was going right. While it may be easy to become discouraged and give up, it is important to remember that life can change in an instant. With the right attitude and a bit of effort, things can turn around quickly. The key is to never give up, no matter how difficult things may seem. Take small steps each day and eventually, you will begin to see progress. Life can indeed go from 0 to 100 real quick – so stay determined, stay focused, and keep pushing forward!

Quitting when the going gets tough is not an option. Everyone experiences challenging times, but it's important to remember that quitting won't get you any closer to success. Instead, it will take you right back to where you began, and you'll be starting all over again. When obstacles arise, don't give up! Persevere and stay focused on your goal. With hard work and dedication, you can achieve anything you set your mind to. Don't forget this important reminder — if you quit now, you won't get anywhere! When you first started out, you may have been desperate to prove yourself right. It can be easy to give up when the going gets tough, but we urge you to keep going! Quitting now will only take you back to where you began, and it won't get you any closer to success. Remind yourself that perseverance pays off in the end, and don't give up on your dreams. With determination and hard work, you can achieve anything!

The old adage "success is not given. It is earned" rings true in many areas of life. Success does not come easy and requires dedication and hard work to achieve. To achieve success, one must set goals, be determined and motivated, and stay focused on the path ahead. There will be obstacles along the way, but with a positive attitude, resilient spirit, and unwavering commitment to success, these can be overcome. By committing to the process of earning success

rather than expecting it to be handed to you, you can lay the foundation for long term achievement.

Life can present us with challenges and struggles that can sometimes seem insurmountable. However, it is important to remember that these difficult days are part of the journey and they can be used to help shape and inform our future. No matter how dark things may seem in the moment, you have to keep pushing forward. When we fight through these tough times, we open ourselves up to new possibilities and opportunities that lead us towards a brighter future. Through our perseverance, we can then earn the best days of our lives.

The old adage, "Be patient. Empires are not built in a day" holds true in all aspects of life. Whether you're building a business, learning a new skill, or working on any other goal it is important to remember that success is often the result of steady and consistent effort over time. It may take months or even years to reach your goals, but with dedication and patience anything is possible. Don't be discouraged if you don't see immediate results; just keep working hard and stay focused on the long-term vision. With the right attitude and approach, you can achieve anything.

It is often said that if you don't do stupid things when you're young, you won't have anything to look back and laugh about when you are older. While it is true that taking risks and making mistakes can lead to some funny memories, it is also important to remember that being reckless in your youth can lead to serious consequences. Taking risks should be done with caution, and if possible, with the guidance of an adult or trusted mentor who can help guide you through making smart decisions. With this in mind, it's possible to find a balance between having fun in your youth and ensuring your safety and future success.

Everyone has goals and dreams that they want to achieve in life. If you are determined enough, nothing can stop you from reaching these goals. With dedication and hard work, anything is possible. Having the right mindset and attitude is key to achieving success; having a positive outlook and believing that you can achieve your goals is essential. It's also important to have a plan of action and to stay focused on the end goal. When faced with setbacks or obstacles, it's important to remain resilient and not give up. By putting in the necessary effort, it's possible to overcome any obstacle and reach your desired destination.

Today, you may be comparing marks with me in school or college. However, one day I will compare my bank balance with yours. This may sound like a joke, but if I am able to properly manage my finances and investments, it is definitely something that I could achieve. It is never too early to start learning about personal finance and investing in order to get ahead. With the right knowledge and discipline, it is possible to build wealth over time and eventually have more financial success than your peers. So let's start today learning how to make smart financial decisions so that one day our bank balances can be compared side-by-side.

It's easy to understand why many people prefer to be in the result rather than in the process. The process often involves a lot of hard work and dedication, while the result is often seen as a reward for all of that effort. Unfortunately, this can create a false sense of security, as it fails to recognize the importance of the journey itself. Being focused on the end result without putting in the work along the way can prevent you from achieving your full potential or reaching your desired goals. Instead, it is important to embrace both the process and the result in order for sustainable success to be achieved.

It's true that a shark in a fish tank will grow to only 8 inches, but in the ocean, it can grow to up to 8 feet or more. This is because of the vast amount of space and resources available in the ocean. Sharks have unlimited room to explore and swim, as well as plenty of food sources, which allow them to reach their full potential size. In contrast, a fish tank is very limited in size and resources. For this reason, it is not able to provide the same amount of growth opportunities for sharks as they would find in their natural environment. Many times, we can find ourselves surrounded by people who think small and are not open to growth. These kinds of individuals can be incredibly detrimental to our personal development, as they stifle our ability to think outside the box. To ensure that you stay motivated and continue to grow, it is important to strive for an environment where your unique perspective is celebrated and encouraged. By surrounding yourself with people who share your enthusiasm for learning and growth, you can create an environment that allows you to reach your highest potential.

It is important to take note of the way people treat us and recognize when we should not tolerate certain behaviors. What we allow speaks volumes about who we are as a person, and it also sets the tone for how other people will interact with us. If we allow ourselves to be treated poorly or in an unprofessional manner, then it sends a message that this type of behavior is acceptable, which can lead to our relationships being based on weak foundations and unhealthy power dynamics. Therefore, it is important to

know what boundaries are necessary to protect ourselves both emotionally and professionally, so that those around us know how we expect to be treated.

Your business is more than a source of income; it is a vehicle that allows you to steer your life to where you want it to go. It can be the foundation for living your life the way you want and thriving in your own unique way. With hard work, dedication, and strategic planning, you can use your business to create the life of your dreams. You'll need to take the time to evaluate all aspects of your business, from marketing and operations, to finance and customer service - ensuring that everything works together in harmony. This will give you greater control over how you use your business as a vehicle for success. By taking charge and having faith in yourself, you can make sure that your business takes you wherever you want it to go.

Financial freedom is the ultimate goal of most people – it means never having to do anything that you don't want to do for money. It comes with a sense of control, creativity and reliability. Achieving financial freedom requires a strategy tailored to your particular goals and lifestyle. This could include cutting spending, building an emergency fund, investing in the stock market or starting a side hustle. Above all, the key is to stay disciplined and focused on achieving

financial freedom, even if it takes time and effort. With dedication and determination, anyone can unlock the doors to financial freedom.

If you don't have passive income rolling into your bank account every month, then it is time to start creating streams of income that will come in even when you don't work. Passive income is money earned from investments that require little or no effort to maintain. This can involve investing in rental properties, dividend stocks, annuities, and other investments that generate a steady flow of cash. To start earning passive income, it is important to identify an investment opportunity that fits your budget and risk tolerance. Research the best options for you and create a plan for generating income over time. With patience and dedication, you can build up a substantial stream of passive income each month.

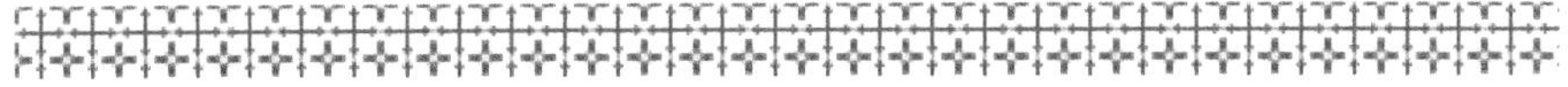

It can be easy to feel overwhelmed by the sheer amount of advice and knowledge on offer when it comes to achieving success. However, if you don't take the time to implement what you have learned, all the strategies, words you have written, or books you have read are essentially useless. To make progress and reach your goals, it is essential that you take action and actually execute your plans. This could mean

setting aside time each day to work on your project or taking small steps every week towards achieving a long-term goal. Whatever it is, taking action is the only way to bring your dreams into reality.

Compounding is a powerful concept that can help you to achieve financial success. The concept of compounding involves reinvesting the returns from previous investments and using them to generate even more returns in the future. For example, if you were to double $0.01 every day for 30 days, by the end of that period you would have accumulated over $5 million - an astonishing return on investment. Compounding works best when done consistently over a long period of time, so it's important to keep investing regularly and reinvesting your returns in order to make the most of this powerful concept.

While it may be tempting to surround yourself with people who are comfortable in their current circumstances and not striving for greatness, it is important that you look for peers on the same mission as you. People who are motivated to continuously improve and reach for their dreams can be an invaluable source of inspiration and motivation. Finding these people and forming meaningful relationships with them can help to keep you focused on your goals and encourage you to stay on track towards achieving them.

It is essential to surround yourself with people who are on the same mission as you. People who are still and lack ambition will bring you down, while those on the same mission can motivate you to keep going and reach your objectives. When selecting your circle of friends, consider the goals and values that they share with you. Look for people who can help to push you forward in life, not hinder your progress. By surrounding yourself with like-minded individuals, you can maintain focus and stay inspired to achieve your goals.

This statement is often used to remind us that there are more important things in life than just material possessions or accumulating wealth. It encourages us to appreciate the non-tangible aspects of our existence such as relationships, experiences, and personal growth. Money can, of course, provide security and the means to live a comfortable life but it should never be our only focus. Living a meaningful and fulfilling life involves having balance in all areas of life including financial security and emotional wellbeing. Ultimately, we must strive to prioritize our well-being over material gain if we want to find true contentment. It is important to remember that there is more to life than just working 40 hours a week in order to get two weeks off a year. It is possible to achieve a good work-life balance without sacrificing your career goals. Taking the time to focus on things you enjoy, like leisure activities, hobbies, and spending time with family and friends can help you regain a sense of balance and perspective. Additionally, taking proactive steps like implementing an effective time management system or learning how to delegate tasks can

give you more control over your workload and free up more of your time for yourself. Ultimately, the key is to find a way to make the most of both your personal and professional commitments without compromising either one.

Selling to potential customers is all about showing them the value you can bring to their life. By understanding their needs and demonstrating how you can make their life easier, you are more likely to make the sale. Make sure that when you are selling, you focus on the benefits that your product or service will provide. This could be anything from saving them time, money or even stress. Show them clearly how what you're offering will improve their current situation and make their life easier. This will help you to convince them of your value and ultimately close the sale. Selling your product or service is all about showing potential customers that you will make their life easier and help them achieve their goals. To do this, you need to clearly communicate the value of your offering. Explain to them why it is beneficial, how it will improve their lives, and what makes it stand out from the competition. Make sure to focus on the customer's needs and interests, rather than just pitching features or touting the quality of your offering. By demonstrating how your product or service can make a positive impact in their life, you can help to increase sales and build lasting relationships with customers.

The key to success is making the right decisions which come from years of experience. Experience teaches us how to recognize opportunities, calculate risks and make informed decisions. Successful people are able to combine their own innate talents with their knowledge and experience, enabling them to make better choices in life. Decisions that are based on experience coupled with a sound knowledge of the world around them are likely to lead to greater success than those made without such guidance. To truly achieve success, it is essential to develop the necessary skills through training and education and then apply those skills by making informed decisions in real-world situations.

It's an age-old saying, "It's lonely at the top." The idea is that when you reach the highest level of success, it can feel lonely, as you have no peers or equals. This idea is reflected in the number of seats that a Bugatti and a bus have. A Bugatti, representing the pinnacle of luxury and exclusivity has only two seats, because there are few people who can truly share in that success. Conversely, a bus has 50 seats to represent the fact that success can be shared with many people, who can help carry you to your goals.

It can be difficult to stay motivated when working towards any goal, but it's your discipline that really makes all the difference. Having a strong motivation will only get you so far if you don't have the necessary discipline to continue through even the most difficult times. Discipline is necessary

for success and it is something that you must cultivate. It means having the same passion and commitment each day, and having the dedication to push yourself even further, no matter how much your motivation may falter along the way. With discipline, you can make sure that you stay on track and reach your goals.

Have you ever felt weak and untrained, lacking the strength and skills to do what you want to do? If so, you aren't alone. But with a little bit of hard work and dedication, you can transform yourself into a stronger and more capable version of yourself. By investing in yourself through proper training and exercise, you can see dramatic improvements in your physical and mental health. Not only will these changes benefit your wellbeing, but they will also give you the strength and courage to pursue bigger dreams and goals. So don't wait any longer - take the first step towards transforming your life today!

If you're between 20 and 30 and your main circle of friends isn't discussing the possibility of opening their own businesses, it can be intimidating to take the first step. However, there are many resources available to help you get started. From seminars to webinars and mentorships to books, there is an abundance of information that can guide you on your entrepreneurial journey. Additionally, you may want to branch out of your main circle and seek out others who have been successful in business. This can provide you with helpful advice as well as a support system that can help keep you motivated when times get tough. Escaping the 9 to 5 and achieving fitness goals can be difficult, but it is possible. One of the key elements to succeeding in these endeavors is having a strong network of support. This

network can provide resources and advice that will help you on your journey, as well as provide encouragement when times get tough. Additionally, having a strong network of contacts can open up opportunities for new ideas and collaborations. Ultimately, "your network is your net worth"– so make sure you make the effort to build relationships with like-minded people.

If you want to be successful and achieve greatness, you must be prepared to face a great deal of criticism and negative feedback. No matter how talented or skilled you are, not everyone will appreciate your success or hard work. You must learn to accept criticism gracefully, use it as motivation to improve, and stay focused on your goals despite the hate. Only then can you truly become great. If you want to be great, you must be prepared to deal with a lot of criticism and hate. It's inevitable that when someone is successful, there will be those who don't understand why and will lash out in resentment. It's important to remember that this is just part of the journey, and it doesn't diminish your accomplishments. In fact, it can even serve as a motivator to keep pushing forward and stay focused on your goals. So if you want to be great, be ready for the haters – but don't let them bring you down.

acquire and it has many benefits. Books are often described as "windows to the world" because they provide access to so much knowledge and information. Reading helps to expand our minds, improves our communication skills, and provides a sense of entertainment. In addition, reading increases our vocabulary, strengthens our memory and concentration, and can even reduce stress. Additionally, reading can help us gain new perspectives and open us up to new ideas. All these factors make it clear why reading is such an important habit to acquire. Reading is an essential part of life and can provide us with many benefits. It allows us to gain knowledge, practice our analytical skills, and expand our imaginations. Reading can also be incredibly enjoyable and even calming. To begin reading more often, start by finding books that you find interesting and that challenge your thinking. Additionally, set a goal for yourself to read a certain number of pages per day or week. When you make reading part of your daily routine, it will soon become a habit that you won't want to break. With the world of information constantly changing, never stop learning by continuing to read new books and articles on topics that interest you.

A successful person is not defined by their outward show of success, but rather by the way they conduct themselves. It is important to remember that success is not a zero-sum game, and there is no need to brag or put down others in order to demonstrate one's own accomplishments. A successful person understands that it is their actions and attitude, not material possessions or outward displays, that truly define them. They strive to set an example for others, using kindness and humility as the foundation for their approach.

By working hard and demonstrating respect for others, a successful person will be able to achieve greater heights of success than those who rely on outward displays alone.

J. K. Rowling is an excellent example of the power of books. After writing the Harry Potter series, she became one of the world's wealthiest authors and a billionaire. Rowling's success demonstrates that books can be incredibly profitable and influential, especially when they have a passionate fanbase. Jeff Bezos is another example of how authors can become wealthy through their work - his company Amazon began as an online bookstore and has since grown to be one of the world's largest companies. Books are powerful tools that can influence individuals, societies, and entire industries. By investing in writing and publishing, authors can make a lasting impact while achieving financial success. Warren Buffett is one of the world's most successful investors and he has achieved great success by reading financial books. By reading and learning from these books, Buffett has been able to gain insight into the market and make informed decisions when it comes to investing. He believes strongly in being an educated investor, as this can help to ensure that his investments are sound and profitable. As such, Warren Buffett has become a billionaire by taking the time to read financial books in order to gain a better understanding of the market.

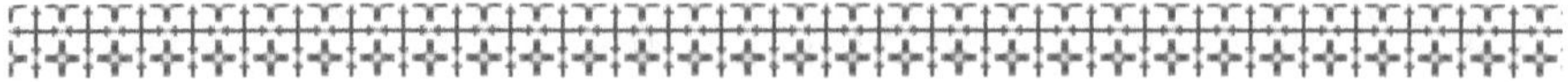

Men in suits are often seen as the epitome of success and authority, but this may not necessarily be the case. It's possible that the men in suits are actually employed by, or working for, someone else. This could be a boss, a mentor, or another figure of power. Regardless of their perceived success, they may still be subject to someone else's authority. This is why it's important to always look beneath the surface and understand what is really going on before making assumptions about those in positions of power. The phrase "men in suits work for the men in pajamas" is sometimes used to describe the modern business environment. It implies that while those in suits—typically senior officials, executives, and other power players—may appear to be the ones calling the shots, they are actually working to serve those wearing more casual attire, such as the employees working from home. This metaphor suggests that even though one group may seem more prominent or powerful than another, all are equally important when it comes to making decisions and running a successful business.

It is often said that a few years of hard work and dedication can lead to a lifetime of freedom. This phrase is particularly applicable to those who are looking to break free from the 9-5 grind and find financial independence. While it may take some time to build up the skills and resources needed to achieve success, the effort you put in now will pay off in the long run. Those who are willing to put in a few years of grinding will find themselves with a lifetime of freedom, be

it financially or otherwise. With hard work and dedication, anything is possible!

The proverb, "Yesterday is history, tomorrow is a mystery but today is a gift. That's why they call it the present", reminds us to make the most of every day. It encourages us to live in the moment and take advantage of the opportunities that present themselves. By embracing each day with enthusiasm and determination, we can ensure that we make the most out of our lives. This can be applied in all aspects of life, from our careers and relationships to our hobbies and spiritual pursuits. In short, this proverb reminds us to be mindful of how precious each day truly is.

This oft-quoted phrase has become increasingly relevant in today's world, as employers are looking for more than just a piece of paper to validate an individual's education and skill set. In addition to academic credentials, employers also want to see evidence of a person's ability to think critically, solve problems, and collaborate effectively with others. This can be demonstrated through one's behavior and communication skills, both at work and in everyday life. A degree may demonstrate knowledge, but behavior is ultimately what sets individuals apart when it comes to demonstrating their education.

The saying "If money can't buy me happiness, I would rather prefer to cry in a Rolls Royce" brings to mind the idea that sometimes the things we think will make us happy, don't actually do so. In this case, the speaker is suggesting that even if material possessions like a fancy car may seem appealing, they cannot truly bring happiness. Instead of investing in material possessions in hopes of gaining contentment, it may be better to focus on cultivating meaningful relationships and experiences. Money can't buy genuine happiness and satisfaction; it's up to us to create our own joy through meaningful experiences.

The best way to get revenge is to move on from whatever has hurt you and continue on a path of success. It is important to take the time to grieve or feel the pain, but ultimately it is best to channel this feeling into motivation for growth and progress. By channeling your energy into productive endeavors, you will be able to achieve success that no one can take away from you. Additionally, it is important to never give up on yourself and remain resilient despite any setbacks or disappointments. Ultimately, by focusing on yourself and your own success, you can find the closure and satisfaction that will be your best revenge. Life can be full of difficult moments, and it is important to remember that you have the power to choose how you will respond to them. Never give someone the satisfaction of watching you suffer. Instead,

take control of your own emotions and reactions. With a positive attitude, you can find ways to turn a difficult situation into an opportunity for growth and learning. When faced with challenging times, remember that you are in control of how you react and ultimately what kind of outcome will result.

It is essential to remember that you can always be replaced. No matter how talented, experienced, or knowledgeable you are at your job, there will always be someone else out there with the same or better qualifications. This serves as an important reminder to stay humble and continue to strive for growth and success in your work. By improving your skills and developing a positive attitude towards work, you can make yourself invaluable in any role. It is also important to remember that no one is irreplaceable, so remain humble and never become complacent in your work.

Many people never take the first step in realizing their dreams and ambitions because they are afraid of what others might think. They lack the confidence to start something from nothing, and the thought of being seen as starting from the bottom is too much for them to bear. Unfortunately, this fear of judgement often prevents people from pursuing their passions and achieving their goals. It is important to remember that there will always be people who criticize what

you are doing, but if you focus on your own growth and progress, it can help to give you the courage to take that first step.

Johnny Kim, aged 36, is living proof that if you dream it, you can do it. Despite being born into a struggling family and facing great hardship in his early years, Johnny worked hard to achieve his dream of becoming a navigator. Through dedication and perseverance, he not only achieved this goal but became one of the most respected navigators in the industry. His story serves as an inspiration to us all that anything is possible with hard work and dedication. He has shown us that no matter what our circumstances may be, if we have a dream we have the power to make it come true.

Everyone has dreams and goals they want to achieve in life. It's important to remember that with hard work and dedication, anything is possible. If you have a dream, it is essential to create achievable goals that will help you get closer to achieving your dream. Set specific timelines and objectives, and be sure to take the necessary steps required to reach your ultimate goal. With a clear vision and determination, you can make your dreams come true!

We all want to be successful, but often times we don't know what it takes to get there. It's easy to come up with a

goal and plan how we want to achieve it, but the reality is that success requires much more than just having a plan. It requires hard work, dedication, and resilience in the face of challenges and setbacks. To truly be successful, you need to have a clear vision of what you want to accomplish, the determination and drive to make it happen, and the willingness to persevere when things don't go according to plan. Success doesn't come easy; it takes commitment, effort, and dedication. With these qualities in place, anything is possible.

Keeping your personal life private is essential for maintaining healthy boundaries in both professional and personal relationships. Your love life, income, and next career move should remain confidential until you are ready to share the information publicly. This is especially true in the workplace, where discussing sensitive topics can lead to rumors and gossip that can damage your reputation. Additionally, talking about these matters prematurely can also lead to disappointment or even conflict if plans don't work out as expected. Keeping these details confidential until the time is right will ensure that you maintain respect and control over such sensitive matters.

The hustle is a part of life for many. You put your head down and work hard, day in and day out, grinding away on

whatever task it is you're trying to accomplish. However, it can be easy to forget to look up every once in a while. When you do look up, you may be surprised at how far you've come in your journey and what you have accomplished. The feeling of amazement when looking back can be an incredible source of motivation that helps keep one pushing forward. Taking the time to reflect on what has been achieved can plant the seeds of inspiration needed to continue striving for more.

Difficult times can teach us some of the most valuable lessons in life. When we go through dark times, it can be difficult to come out of them and move on with our lives. However, it is important to recognize that these difficult experiences have made us stronger, wiser and better prepared for the future. That's why you should never regret what you went through but instead take the time to appreciate all the valuable lessons learned during these dark times. By doing so, you can find strength to move forward and make the best of your current situation. No one likes to go through difficult times, but it is important to remember that these experiences can teach us valuable lessons. During dark times, we often learn more about ourselves than ever before. We learn self-discipline and resilience, along with the power of gratitude and the importance of surrounding ourselves with positive people. Instead of becoming bitter or resentful, we should focus on being thankful for all the lessons our dark times have taught us. These lessons can help us be better prepared for any future challenges that come our way.

Entrepreneurship knows no age, and the youngest entrepreneurs are proving that success can come at any age. From Mark Zuckerberg to Bill Gates, there are countless examples of young entrepreneurs who have achieved great success. No matter your age, the key to success is to be so good that they can't ignore you. It takes dedication, hard work and a willingness to learn in order to create something remarkable; but if you stay focused on your goal then anything is possible. So if you want to become an entrepreneur – don't let your age stop you! Be so good that they can't ignore you, and keep chasing after your dreams until they become reality.

Age is nothing but a number and it should not be used as a limitation for success. Just look at the example of Elon Musk and Mark Zuckerberg who both achieved incredible things from a young age. At 12 years old, Elon Musk sold his first computer game, Blastar, while Mark Zuckerberg built a program he called ZuckNet at the age of 12. Both of these accomplishments demonstrate that you don't need to be an adult in order to be successful, and that age should not be seen as an obstacle to achieving your goals.

Innovating is not for the faint of heart. It takes courage, tenacity and an unwavering commitment to the idea. Despite this, when you decide to innovate, you'll have to be prepared for people telling you that you are crazy, out of your mind or otherwise "nuts". It is important to approach this criticism

by remembering that it could just be people's way of expressing their discomfort with change and unfamiliar concepts. Don't let it stop you from pushing ahead and continuing on your innovative journey.

No matter how hard it is, embracing the storms in life is essential for growth. Without rain, plants cannot grow — they need water and nourishment to thrive. Similarly, we need difficult situations and hardships to cultivate our strength and resilience. Difficult times give us the opportunity to learn and grow, to develop courage and patience. It's important to remember that every storm will eventually pass, as long as you have the courage and persistence to see it through. By learning to embrace the storms of life you can open yourself up for greater growth and success.

When you truly want something, you have to go after it without limiting yourself with doubts, fears, and insecurities. When you make an effort to reach your goals, despite any obstacles that come your way, you will be able to manifest what you desire. It is important to stay focused and motivated throughout the process, since it is easy to get discouraged when things don't go as planned. It also helps to surround yourself with positive people who will support and encourage you on this journey. With a clear vision and

the right attitude, anything is possible! the power of positive thinking and action. When you put your heart and soul into wanting something, the universe will respond. By taking steps towards achieving your greatest desires and believing in yourself, the universe will provide you with the resources and opportunities you need to make it happen. This could mean anything from finding a new job opportunity to meeting a special someone or accomplishing a difficult task. When you truly want something , the universe will make it happen.

With seven billion people on the planet, it is easy to see the potential for what we can accomplish if we all come together. If we were to replace feelings of animosity or distrust with love and respect, our collective power would be amplified. We could build a world where everyone is given equitable opportunities, and each person's individual strengths are recognized. We could use our combined resources to tackle some of the most pressing global issues facing us today. Imagine what seven billion humans can accomplish if we all loved and respected one another - anything is possible!

Money speaks only one language: If you save me today, I will save you tomorrow. This phrase is a reminder of the importance of saving money and making wise financial decisions. Saving money today can have a positive impact on

your future, allowing you to take advantage of opportunities that may come your way. It can also help to avoid financial hardship by providing funds for unexpected expenses or emergencies. By setting aside money each month and investing it in safe and secure options, you can ensure that money will be available when you need it most. Investing for the future requires discipline and commitment, but it can pay off in the long run.

Going through training can be a difficult process, especially if you don't enjoy the subject matter or the tasks. However, it is important to stay motivated and remain dedicated to your goal no matter how tedious the training may seem. I hated every minute of my training, but I reminded myself that in the end it would all be worth it. Even when things began to get overwhelming, I said "don't quit" and kept pushing myself until I had completed my training.

This famous quote from Muhammad Ali is a powerful reminder of the importance of hard work and perseverance. Everyone has to suffer difficult moments in their lives, but by embracing these challenges and seeing them as an opportunity to grow, we can transform them into life-defining moments that shape us into champions. It's easy to get discouraged when facing tough times, but if we can push through and remain focused on our goals, then the rewards are worth the pain.

One of the biggest mistakes we make is assuming that other people think the same way as we do. We often forget that everyone processes information differently, and what makes sense in our minds may not make sense to someone else. This can lead to misunderstandings and frustrations when communicating with others. We need to be aware of this tendency and take the time to consider how others may perceive or interpret our messages. By doing so, we can create more meaningful connections with others and foster better relationships built on mutual understanding and respect.

Have you ever wondered why the very last person on your mind before you fall asleep is either the reason for your happiness or unhappiness? This phenomenon is one of the most common questions asked by those who are struggling to maintain a healthy balance between their personal and professional lives. On one hand, it can be comforting to think about someone who brings joy and light into our lives. On the other hand, it can be difficult to process intense emotions such as anger or sadness when this same person is the last thing we think of before falling asleep. It is important to remember that these thoughts will pass and that we can use our minds to focus on more positive things in order to help us get a good night's rest.

Every day is a new chance to start fresh and strive to become a better version of yourself. Life is full of surprises, so it's important to make the most of each day. You can start by setting small, achievable goals that will help you reach your big-picture goals. This could include something as simple as reading a few pages in a self-improvement book, learning a new skill, or taking steps towards pursuing your dreams. Every little step counts, and by making use of each day's opportunities, you can slowly but surely transform into the best version of yourself.

It's easy to forget that the biggest obstacle to success isn't other people, but rather our own procrastination. When we procrastinate, it not only keeps us from achieving our goals, but it also prevents us from learning and growing. It's important to recognize that we are our own worst enemies and that the only way to be successful is to outrun our own procrastination. This can be done by taking small steps each day towards achieving our goals and staying focused on the big picture. By doing this, we can stay ahead of ourselves and ultimately beat out any competition. We often think of competition as being against other people, whether in work, sports, or life in general. However, the most formidable opponent we can face is our own ego. While it may be tempting to compare ourselves to others and try to compete with them, focusing on our own goals and personal bests can be more rewarding. We should strive to challenge ourselves and push beyond our limits rather than trying to measure up against someone else's accomplishments. By channeling

our competitive spirit into challenging our own egos, we can unlock even greater potential and open the door for personal growth and development.

The old adage of "if you ask for help they laugh, do it yourself and they hate" is a common refrain in life. It can be easy to take this advice to heart, but it is important to remember that asking for help is simply part of the learning process. When done correctly, asking for assistance can provide valuable insight and can even lead to a better end result. Moreover, learning from an expert or mentor can provide knowledge that would not be accessible otherwise. While the saying may have some merit, if done thoughtfully and respectfully, asking for help should not be something to fear or avoid.

It's easy to talk the talk and say you want something, but it's a completely different story when it comes to actually putting in the hard work and effort to achieve it. Many people think they want something until the reality of what it takes to make it happen sets in—which is usually when they realize that their dreams may be out of reach. It takes courage, determination, and dedication to persevere in spite of any obstacles that may stand in your way. If you truly want something, you have to be willing to do whatever it takes to make it happen. Making a committed decision

upfront is essential for achieving success in any endeavor. This means that you need to be willing to do whatever it takes to reach your goal. Whether it's studying hard, making sacrifices, or dedicating extra time and energy, commitment is key when it comes to achieving success. Having the right attitude and dedication will always pay off in the end, so be sure to make the necessary commitment before you start on your journey.

It is easy to get caught up in worrying about what other people think of you and your opinions. However, it is important to remember that the most important opinion is your own. It doesn't matter if somebody else can't see what you do or understand why you think a certain way - the only thing that matters is that you are true to yourself. You should always believe in yourself and trust your instincts, even if that means going against the grain. Having faith in yourself and following your intuition will lead you to success and satisfaction, no matter what anyone else may think.

Your circle of friends, family, and other close connections should be a source of pride. This means that they should be supportive and encouraging, not competitive or jealous. Jealousy can lead to resentment, which can damage relationships in your circle. Instead, focus on creating an environment where everyone is free to express themselves

and their accomplishments without fear of judgement or comparison. Celebrate each other's successes and work together to create a positive atmosphere where everyone feels accepted and appreciated for who they are.

Many people believe that experience and age necessarily go hand in hand. It is assumed that the more years a person has lived, the more experience they have. However, this isn't necessarily the case. Living the same number of years may not equate to having the same level of experience as another person. Factors such as one's individual learning capacity, their dedication to self-improvement and development, and even external influences can all play a role in determining how much a person has learned in a given amount of time. Ultimately, age alone cannot be used as an accurate measure of experience or knowledge.

It is often said that talent is something that you are born with and cannot be developed. However, this is not necessarily true. While some people may have a natural inclination or aptitude for certain activities, the truth is that hard work and dedication can help to hone and refine any skill. In fact, it could be argued that talent without hard work can never truly reach its full potential. If you are passionate about something and are willing to put in the effort to improve your craft, then you will be able to develop

your own unique talent - no matter how great or small it may be. So while talent may be important, hard work and dedication should never be underestimated.

The fear of waking up and going to work for someone else's business is a common one. Whether it's the fear of being stuck in a job you don't enjoy or the fear of not having enough control over your work, it can be daunting to have someone else dictate your day-to-day. This fear can lead to feelings of anxiety, depression, and even insomnia. It can also lead to procrastination and stagnation in both our professional and personal lives. It is important that we recognize this fear and take steps to manage it in order to reach our goals and live the life we want. Taking small steps towards establishing financial independence or creating a side hustle can help us feel more empowered over our lives. For many, the prospect of spending forty years in someone else's business can be a scary thought. It's a fear that many don't want to face — after all, who wants to be stuck in someone else's job for that long? The idea of being in an unfulfilling, unmotivating career for such a long period can be daunting. Nevertheless, it is important to remember that there are ways to make sure this worst-case scenario doesn't happen. With the right career planning and self-awareness, you can ensure that you will wake up everyday feeling fulfilled and motivated. It is essential to be aware of your own values, goals and interests so you can create a plan.

Some people talk to you in their free time because they enjoy having conversations with you. They want to get to know more about you, share stories, and just generally connect with you. On the other hand, some people need to "free their time"—they need to feel like they have enough space and freedom to express themselves, without worrying about taking up too much of your time. This doesn't mean that these people don't care about you—it just means that they need a little extra room and understanding when it comes to communication. Learning how to balance both types of behavior is key in any relationship.

Knowing that you are truly self-made is one of the greatest feelings of satisfaction in life. It means that you have been able to achieve success and reach your goals using your own skills, talents, and abilities. This sense of accomplishment and pride can be incredibly rewarding, as it comes from within rather than from external sources. With a self-made mindset, you can go further than you ever thought possible and gain a deeper appreciation for what you have achieved. You also gain a greater appreciation for the journey it took to get there, as well as the dedication and hard work required to make it happen. Knowing that you are self-made is a feeling that will stay with you forever – one that will bring joy not just today but also in their future endevours.

Isolation is an important factor when it comes to the birth of ideas. When we are in a quiet and peaceful environment, our thoughts can flow freely and without interruption. This allows us to explore possibilities and develop creative solutions that may not have been thought of in a crowded or noisy environment. By isolating ourselves from distraction, we create a space where ideas can grow and flourish. Ultimately, this can lead to greater success in our work and life endeavors.

In 2004, Mark Zuckerberg famously dropped out of Harvard University just two years into his studies. Despite this, he returned to Harvard in 2017 to receive an honorary degree. By the time of the graduation ceremony, Zuckerberg had already become a billionaire thanks to his success with Facebook. This made him one of the richest people in the world and an example of how a college education is not always necessary for success. In his speech at the ceremony, Zuckerberg urged graduates to think about using their skills for creating positive change in the world.

It is often said that a degree is not necessary to become successful, and while this may be true in some cases, it is a dangerous oversimplification. A degree can provide valuable skills and knowledge that can open doors to career opportunities and give individuals an edge over their competition. However, even with a degree it still takes hard work and dedication to achieve success; a degree does not guarantee success in any way. Ultimately, the combination of education and hard work will help create the best path for each individual to reach their goals.

Everything in life is about priorities, and what you prioritize will dictate the outcome of any situation. Whether it's making decisions in your personal or professional life, setting clear priorities can help you to stay focused and achieve your goals. When deciding what to prioritize, it's important to consider both long-term and short-term objectives. If you focus only on short-term tasks, you may not be able to make progress towards your bigger goals. On the other hand, if you focus too much on long-term goals, you may miss out on opportunities that can help you reach those goals more quickly. By taking the time to think about your priorities and plan accordingly, you can create a plan for success that will keep you motivated and on track.

You know what your problem is? You're SMART. Too SMART. You overthink because you have the ability to, but this can often lead to analysis paralysis and prevent you from taking action on important tasks. Overthinking can lead to stress, anxiety, and a feeling of being overwhelmed by your own thoughts and ideas. To combat this issue, it is important to recognize when you are overthinking and take steps to manage it. Understanding that the time you spend overthinking is taking away from productive time will

help motivate you to take action and make decisions without getting lost in your own mind. Additionally, it may be helpful to practice mindfulness or meditation as a way of calming your mind and managing stress levels. Taking the time each day.

Rowan Atkinson, the British actor, comedian and writer, was rejected by many television shows due to his stammering. Despite his success in theater and radio, it took him several years before he got his first break in television. This was due to his speech impediment which caused him to struggle with speaking fluently. He eventually found success on television with his classic roles in Mr Bean and Blackadder, becoming one of the UK's most beloved comedians. Today, Rowan is recognised for his genius comic timing which often masks the fact that he still struggles to speak fluently. His story is an inspiring reminder that sometimes our greatest gifts come from our biggest challenges.

Greed is a strong motivator that can drive us to make decisions with our hard-earned money that are not always in our best interest. In the heat of the moment, we may be willing to take on more risk than we would normally be comfortable with in order to chase a higher return. We can also fall into the trap of making impulse purchases without considering all aspects of an investment or purchase, such

as fees and taxes. Greed can lead us down a dangerous path, so it is important to practice financial discipline and think carefully before making any decision with your hard-earned money.

The people who are crazy enough to think that they can change the world are the ones who usually end up doing it. They are not afraid to take risks, to challenge the status quo, and to believe in themselves and their ideas. They recognize that failure is part of the process and know that if they keep trying, eventually something will work. This kind of courage and commitment is what sets these individuals apart from those who just talk about making a difference but never actually take action. Those who are crazy enough to think they can change the world understand that success is possible, even when it seems impossible.

The 50/30/20 rule is an easy way to prioritize and budget your money. Under this rule, you should set aside 50% of your income for needs like rent, bills, and groceries. The other 30% should go towards wants like going out to dinner or buying new clothes. Finally, the remaining 20% should be set aside for savings or financial goals. By setting up a budget using the 50/3/20 rule, you can make sure that your spending stays on track while still allowing yourself some room to splurge from time to time.

The saying "for your income to change, your mindset has to change" holds true in many areas of life. This is especially relevant to those looking to increase their income and become financially successful. In order to reach a higher level of financial success, it is important to have the right mindset and focus on achieving goals. By setting realistic goals and working towards them with fortitude, you can gradually increase your income over time. Additionally, developing positive habits such as budgeting and saving can help you reach your goals faster and more effectively. With the right attitude, determination, and strategies in place, anyone can make positive changes in their financial life.

Comfort zones can provide a sense of security and familiarity in life, but it's important to recognize when it's time to leave that zone. Comfort zones can often be too

comfortable, leading us to stay in the same place for too long and not challenge ourselves. By pushing the boundaries of our comfort zones and taking risks, we can open ourselves up to new experiences and opportunities for growth. It is important to weigh the pros and cons of leaving your comfort zone, but by doing so we can learn more about ourselves and even discover hidden talents. Taking a step outside of our comfort zone helps us expand our horizons and develop as individuals.

Mansa Musa was a 14ᵗʰ-century ruler of the Mali Empire, which at the time was one of the largest and richest empires in Africa. He is widely regarded as the wealthiest person to have ever lived and his wealth was built on gold, salt, and other natural resources that were abundant in Mali. Mansa Musa's legacy includes not only his wealth but also his religious piety, as he made extensive donations to Islamic shrines throughout his empire. He also built extensive public works projects in Mali, such as mosques and schools, in order to promote Islam and advance education. To this day Mansa Musa remains an important figure of African culture and is remembered for his contributions to both religion and society.

Blaming someone for your life's struggles is an easy trap to fall into, but ultimately it can be a fruitless exercise. Instead

of placing blame on someone else, focus on the steps you can take to make improvements in your life. It's true that good people can bring joy and happiness, while bad people can bring grief and sadness. But what's important is that you learn from your experiences with everyone in your life and use the lessons you have learned to move forward. Don't get stuck in the past - look ahead to the future and focus on making positive changes that will help you reach your goals.

It is often easy to get overwhelmed when trying to make big changes in our lives, but it is important to remember that small changes always eventually lead to big results. Taking small steps and making consistent progress towards a goal will always pay off in the end. The real Zack Smith, an entrepreneur with a successful business and motivational speaker, is a testament to this fact. He was able to achieve success by taking small actions every day that eventually compounded into big results over time. It is also important to note that we must remain consistent with these small changes if we want them to add up over time. By finding ways to incorporate small actions into our daily routines, we can create lasting change and ultimately achieve the results we desire.

We all have a picture-perfect image of ourselves that we project to the world. We want others to believe that we are

put-together, successful, and perfect in every way. However, behind this facade is often a messy truth. We all have struggles that we may not be open about; from issues with self-confidence to depression and anxiety. It is important to remember that no one is perfect and that everyone has their own struggles and messiness beneath the surface. By recognizing this in ourselves and in others, we can create a more supportive environment for all.

Having a job can feel like carrying heavy water buckets your whole life. You are constantly working to make ends meet, and even when you do, it can be difficult to get ahead financially. Owing assets such as a house or car can also feel like a weight around your neck. These items require upkeep and maintenance that can easily deplete your budget. Despite the challenges, having a job and owning assets is essential for achieving long-term security and financial stability. With thoughtful budgeting and saving strategies, you can build wealth over time without feeling overwhelmed by the amount of work required to maintain them.

Our minds are powerful tools and can either be used to our benefit or detriment. In order to ensure that our minds are an asset, we need to be mindful of what we feed it. This includes the information and thoughts we take in from outside sources as well as the dialogue we have with

ourselves. By being aware of the messages we are receiving and implementing positive self-talk, we can turn our minds into a formidable asset that will help us achieve our goals. Additionally, engaging in activities such as mindfulness and meditation can help us become more aware of our thoughts and clear away negative mental blocks so that they no longer stand in our way. When used correctly, your mind can be your greatest asset, so don't let it become your liability.

Luxury brands often have a set pricing strategy and stick to it regardless of their customers' budgets. This is because luxury brands need to maintain their status as high-end products, and the price is an integral part of this. For example, if a luxury product was significantly discounted, it might take away from its exclusivity and perceived value in the market. For this reason, many luxury brands opt to set their prices higher than those of competitors in order to preserve their brand image and attract wealthy customers who can afford them.

An investment is an asset or item that is purchased with the goal of generating income or appreciating in value over time. Usain Bolt, the world's fastest man, ran a 100m sprint in less than 115 seconds. He achieved this remarkable feat by investing a tremendous amount of time and effort into training and preparation - he trained for more than 20 hours

a week in order to reach this level of performance. Investing in yourself can take on many forms, and it's important to recognize the value of these investments. It may not always be easy, but if you put in the right amount of effort, you can achieve amazing results like Usain Bolt did.

Inflation is a silent killer, as the cost of living rises over time and erodes the value of your money. As such, it is important to always invest your money in order to beat inflation. Investing can include putting your money into stocks, bonds, mutual funds, or even real estate. With the right strategy, you can ensure that your wealth grows over time while maintaining its purchasing power. Investing in these vehicles can help you counteract the effects of inflation and protect your financial future. Inflation is a natural part of the economy and it can be difficult to keep your money safe from its effects. However, investing your money is one of the best ways to beat inflation and keep your wealth secure. When you invest in stocks, bonds, mutual funds and other financial instruments, your money can increase in value while still maintaining its purchasing power. This means that you won't have to worry about inflation reducing the value of your investments over time. In addition to helping you protect yourself against inflation, investing can also help you build wealth and achieve financial goals. Whether you are looking to save for retirement or simply grow your savings over time, investing can be an effective way to reach your financial goals.

We all make mistakes, but it's important to remember the lesson, not the disappointment of making the mistake. Instead of trying to erase your mistake, focus on the learning experience and how you can use that knowledge in the future. This will help you to become a stronger and more resilient person in the long run, as well as a more successful one. By taking away the focus from your failure and remembering the lesson instead, you will be able to move forward with confidence and optimism.

If you are serious about making a lasting change in your life, then you have to be willing to go through uncomfortable situations. Change is rarely easy and often requires us to push ourselves outside of our comfort zone. This could mean taking risks, speaking up when we normally wouldn't, or facing our fears. It is only through these moments of discomfort that true transformation can occur. So if you are serious about change, it is important to be mindful of the steps you take and the situations that make you uncomfortable as they could be exactly what will move you towards a better future.

It's easy to get caught up in the day-to-day grind of life and neglect the bigger picture. We often try to take shortcuts, seeking quick solutions that promise big results with minimal effort. However, this approach often fails to produce lasting results and can even lead to failure in the long run. The only way to achieve real growth is by embracing the process; by taking a step back and acknowledging that progress is best made through consistent, hard work rather than trying to find a shortcut or dodge the process. It may not be glamorous, but it's the only way to truly grow and reach your fullest potential.

The key to success is to stay focused on improving and developing yourself, rather than getting distracted by the things around you. It's important to make time for self-improvement so that you can become the best version of yourself. By dedicating time to studying, learning, practicing and developing your skills and abilities, you can grow both professionally and personally. Focusing on personal growth also leaves less time for distractions and prevents you from becoming complacent. So remember to be so busy improving yourself that you don't have time to pay attention to anything else.

Everyone is important and has their own unique purpose in life. We all have different gifts and abilities that make us special, and it is important to recognize this. Everyone can contribute something meaningful in the world, no matter how small it may seem. It is also important to realize that everyone matters and has the potential to make an impact in their own unique way. By valuing individual contributions and recognizing everyone's importance, we are creating a more inclusive environment where everyone feels respected

and appreciated.

This popular saying is a reminder to not underestimate others and to instead approach each person with respect. It serves as a reminder that everyone is unique and has something to offer, regardless of what they may appear to be on the surface. Taking the time to admire someone's shoes is an easy way to show appreciation for another person's individual style and identity. It also serves as a reminder that it's important to treat others with kindness, even if you don't have anything in common. By looking past appearances and taking time to get to know someone, we can all make the world a kinder place.

The razor blade and the axe are two common tools used for cutting. While both have their advantages, they also have their limits. The razor blade is extremely sharp and can make precision cuts in many materials. However, it is unable to cut through something as tough as a tree trunk. Similarly, the axe is strong enough to split wood, but it cannot cut hair-thin lines like the razor blade can. Understanding these limitations is key to using each tool appropriately and efficiently.

It is important to retain a sense of respect in all that we do. Respect for not just ourselves and our beliefs, but also for the people and things around us. We should always try to go above and beyond when it comes to treating others with kindness and love, as well as respecting their opinions and feelings even if it differs from our own. At the same time, however, we must never let our respect die. We should strive to maintain an attitude of respect even when we are feeling frustrated or angry. In this way, we can show others that we still value them even when they do not agree with us. Doing so can help foster strong relationships between people and encourage mutual understanding and appreciation.

The phrase "Not every closed door is locked. PUSH." can be interpreted in many different ways, but its overall meaning is that if you want something, you have to take the initiative and put in the effort to make it happen. It encourages us to push past any barriers that may be standing in our way and not give up when faced with challenges. Taking risks and trying something new can lead to great opportunities and success, so it's important to remain persistent and keep pushing forward despite any closed doors that may appear along the way.

Sometimes the best way to get what you want is to push hard. This doesn't mean you have to be aggressive or obnoxious — simply be persistent in your approach. If someone is resistant to your requests, don't give up. Try a different tack, or come back with a stronger argument. Ultimately, it's important to stay positive and understand that not everyone is going to be receptive to your ideas right off the bat. If you can keep a positive attitude and continue to push, eventually you will get what you want.

This is a mantra that we should all live by, especially when it comes to life's difficult moments. Even when the world is not recognizing the good you do, know that it does not mean you should give up on yourself or your goals. It takes courage and resilience to keep pushing forward despite the odds, and it is especially important to remember this during times of criticism. Life will always have its ups and downs, but you can count on yourself to always make sure you are pushing forward in the right direction.

It's a sad reality that the world can often be unappreciative of the good deeds you do. You could try your best to help someone out or donate your time and money to a worthy cause, yet you may not receive any acknowledgement for it. Unfortunately, it's been said that people will forget the thousand acts of kindness but remember one mistake you make. Instead of worrying about what other people think, focus on living with integrity and using your experiences to grow. Your true reward will come from knowing that you have done something good with your life. While it can be difficult to stay strong in the face of criticism and laughter, it is essential to remain focused on your goals and objectives. No matter what kind of adversity you face, keep in mind that there is always a way to overcome it and find success if you put your mind to it. When faced with heavy criticism or ridicule, remember that you have the power to rise above it

and remain confident in yourself and your abilities. Be sure to take the time for self-care, as this can help build resilience in times of difficulty. It is also important to surround yourself with supportive people who will help lift you up when times get tough. Ultimately, remember that staying strong when faced with difficult situations will help set you apart from the rest of the world.

This quote speaks to the power of faith and resilience in difficult times. When it may seem like nothing is happening, and there is no light at the end of the tunnel, it is important to remember that God is always at work. We cannot see all the moving pieces, but God has a plan that only He can see. So even when things seem still and hopeless, we must trust in His plan and remain in faith.

Once you set your mind on the right path, the possibilities are endless. Having the right attitude and approach can make all the difference towards achieving your goals and dreams. It is important to focus on what you want to achieve and stay determined despite obstacles and challenges that you may encounter. You must be willing to put in the hard work and dedication needed to make it happen. With a strong mindset and positive outlook, anything can be accomplished - so set your sights high, work hard, and never give up!

The phrase "you can fool everybody, except the man in the mirror" is an age-old proverb that serves as a reminder to be honest with yourself and take responsibility for your actions. It speaks to the idea that trying to deceive others may be successful for a time, but ultimately you will know in your heart if you are being honest or not. This proverb encourages individuals to be true to themselves and uphold their values, even when it may be easier to take the easy way out. It also serves as a warning that people should not be too quick to trust those who seem too good to be true - because often times they are.

Working on yourself every single day is an important part of personal growth and development. It can involve anything from learning a new skill to taking time for yourself each

day to reflect and rejuvenate. Working on yourself does not have to be time consuming or expensive, it can be as simple as setting aside 10 minutes per day for self-care or spending an hour each week reading a book that you find inspiring. Whatever it is that you choose to focus on, the most important thing is to dedicate yourself to doing something that helps you grow and develop as a person. With consistent effort, you can make incredible strides in your personal growth and development over time.

The odds of you being born as you are are one in four trillion, making your existence truly remarkable. Not only did the stars have to align for you to be born; countless generations of your ancestors and countless other factors had to be just right for you to come into this world. It is easy to take our lives for granted and forget how special it is that we were able to exist at all, especially in light of the improbability of it all. Your life is a testament not only to you and your family, but also to the laws of nature that made your unique existence possible.

The idea that there is no ultimate destination and that the journey is everything has been around for centuries. It encourages us to enjoy the present moment, appreciate the little things and to focus on the process rather than worrying about the outcome. By understanding that our lives are made

up of different experiences and moments, we can find joy in every step of our journey, regardless of the destination. This philosophy can be seen in many aspects of life: from taking time to savor a delicious meal, to enjoying a leisurely stroll through nature, or even pursuing a lifelong passion. Each moment has something to offer and when we embrace this idea, we can find fulfillment in every part of our lives.

Life is naturally what we make it. We have the power to create our own paradises or our own nightmares. It is up to us to decide and take action on how we want to live life. Life is not inherently good or bad, it all starts with us. We must take the right steps and make an effort to improve our lives if we want life to become a paradise. This requires hard work, dedication, goal setting and taking steps every day towards improving our lives. Whether this means finding new hobbies, learning new skills or creating healthier habits – having an intention and a plan will help you in changing your life from Crap to Paradise.

"What you truly believe about yourself determines who you will become." This phrase is an important reminder that the beliefs we hold about ourselves can have a huge influence on our lives and our ultimate success. Our self-beliefs shape our thoughts, feelings, and behaviors in ways that either propel us towards our goals or lead us down paths of stagnation

or even failure. It is essential to recognize that believing in oneself has the power to unlock potential and create lasting change. This means investing time and effort into creating positive, empowering beliefs about ourselves that are based on reality rather than outdated ideas or negative self-talk. Doing so will help to create a foundation for success, no matter what challenge we may face.

In today's competitive and fast-paced world, it can be tempting to take the quickest path to success. Although there may be short-term gains from a quick success, it usually does not last. When success is achieved through hard work and determination, however, it can build character and resilience. Slow success builds character by teaching perseverance, patience, and dedication; fast success builds the ego by creating a false sense of invincibility. Slow success is more fulfilling in the long run, as it instills the qualities necessary for long-term growth and development.

It is true that the world around us will judge us based on how we view and present ourselves. We must learn to be kind to ourselves and think positively if we want others to see us in a positive light. It is important to remember that no matter what other people may think of us, our own opinion of ourselves should always be the strongest and most important one. Thinking positively can help us stay motivated and have

more confidence in our abilities. We should strive for self-compassion and recognize that mistakes are part of life, allowing us to learn from them and grow. By looking at ourselves through a positive lens, we can create a bright future for ourselves and those around us.

It can be difficult to cut ties with people who make us feel like we don't deserve a good life. However, it is important to realize that these people are not serving us in our journey towards success and happiness. In order to move forward, we must be willing to let go of the strings tying us down. This will free up our energy and allow us to focus on what truly matters: ourselves. The decision to cut strings may be painful in the short term, but it will ultimately lead to greater joy and fulfillment in the long run.

Having the right mindset is essential when it comes to achieving your goals and dreams. It's not just about having a positive attitude, but instead, having a growth mindset that allows you to learn from mistakes and see challenges as opportunities. Working on developing this mindset can help you stay motivated and focused on reaching your goals, even when faced with obstacles. Cultivating this mindset will also help you stay committed, because you trust that each step is taking you closer to success. Thus, by focusing on developing the right mindset, you will be better equipped to reach your

goals and dreams.

When nails grow long, it is important to remember the proverb 'we cut nails not fingers'. This proverb highlights that it is best to take care when cutting long nails, as we want to avoid any accidental cuts or injuries to ourselves. It reminds us that we should always be careful and practice good hygiene when cutting our own nails or those of another person. Taking this into consideration will help us to maintain healthy, well-manicured nails without any unnecessary risks.

Misunderstandings can arise in any relationship. It is important to remember that when those misunderstandings arise, it is best to take a step back and try to see the situation from both perspectives. Cutting your ego out of the equation and focusing on resolving the misunderstanding with respect and understanding can go a long way towards preserving a healthy relationship. Instead of lashing out at each other or taking an "I'm right, you're wrong" approach, try to come to an agreement that satisfies both parties. It may take more effort on your part, but it will be worth it in the long run for your relationship.

Training your brain is just as important as training your body when it comes to achieving success. Your mind is your

biggest asset, and neglecting it can lead to stagnation and dissatisfaction with life. Just as you would with physical exercise, make sure you take time every day to focus on mental development. This can include reading inspiring books and articles, practicing mindfulness or meditation, or engaging in thought-provoking conversations with others. Taking the time to train your brain will pay off in the long run, allowing you to reach your highest potential and live a life of purposeful growth and fulfillment.

No matter what you do, your work and effort should never be something to be ashamed of. Too often we can feel embarrassed or ashamed of ourselves when our work is not as successful as we would like it to be, but it's important to remember that success is not a guarantee. Hard work and hustle are the only things that are going to bring you success in the long run, and if you don't put in the effort, then no one else is going to pick up the slack for you. Nobody will feed you if you go broke, so always strive for success and never give up on yourself.

Sometimes, when we are searching for something in life, it can be difficult to find exactly what we're looking for. After much time and effort spent looking in the wrong places, we may finally realize that what we have been searching for was right in front of us all along. This could be a person, a job

opportunity, or any other form of fulfillment that we have been seeking. The takeaway from this is that it's important to take the time to really evaluate all possibilities before making a decision. Taking the time to really consider our options is essential if we want to make sure that we find exactly what it is that has been missing in our lives.

It can be hard to see the lessons in our losses and mistakes, but it's important to remember that we're not always right. In life, we need feedback and guidance to help us improve and grow. When people kick us while we're down, it can be a sign that they care about our future success. Instead of resenting them for their criticism, take it as an opportunity to re-evaluate your path, make changes where necessary, and push yourself further than ever before. Being thankful for those who have kicked you while you were down is a great way to ensure that you keep reaching higher heights in life.

In life, it's important to be thankful for where you are now and keep fighting for where you want to be tomorrow. Although it can be easy to focus on the things that we don't have, it's important to recognize all of the good that surrounds us. Being thankful for our current circumstances doesn't mean that we should stop striving for more. On the contrary, it is by being grateful for what we already have that we are able to keep pushing forward and remain motivated

in our journey towards our goals. So take a moment today to appreciate all of your blessings, and use them as motivation to keep striving towards greater success.

When it comes to achieving our dreams, it can be difficult to separate ourselves from the crowd and find our own unique path. However, this is often necessary in order to make our dreams a reality. It takes courage and determination to break away from what's comfortable and familiar, but it is essential if you want to succeed. Instead of following the path laid out for us by society, take the time to consider what makes your dreams different than everyone else's. Develop a plan that is tailored specifically to your goals and put in the hard work necessary for success. With a clear vision and dedication, you will be able to make your dreams come true.

It's true that not all people in your life are meant to stay there forever. Over time, some connections may become strained or simply drift apart as life moves on and things change. But it's important to remember that even when a person isn't in your life anymore, they weren't necessarily a "friend." Sometimes, the people we think are our friends turn out to be undercover haters, and it can take time to recognize their true intentions. Real friends—the ones who have your best interests at heart and genuinely care about you—can never be lost. If a person really cares about you,

they will always remain present in some form or another.

Your salary can be a hindrance to achieving your dreams and goals. It is easy for us to become accustomed to our current salary and adjust our lifestyle accordingly. This can lead us to settle into a routine that doesn't allow for the pursuit of new opportunities or the growth of our skills. It is important to remember that it is possible to use our salary as a tool, rather than an obstacle, in order to pursue our dreams. By being mindful of how we spend our salary and setting aside money for savings, we open up the possibility of pursuing new opportunities with increased financial security.

The famous quote "Today's pain becomes tomorrow's power" is a reminder that every difficult experience we go through can be transformed into something that strengthens us and makes us better. Painful situations can teach us valuable lessons and help us to grow. Though it may not feel like it in the moment, it is possible to see beyond our current struggles and to recognize the power they have to shape the future. By looking at our experiences with this mindset, we can find courage, resilience, and hope in even the darkest of times.

Deciding what you want and writing it down is the first step in achieving any goal. Once you have an idea of what you want to accomplish, create a plan detailing exactly how to get there. Break it down into smaller goals that are achievable within a certain timeframe, and create an actionable plan for each one. Finally, make sure to work on your plan every day, no matter how small the task. This will ensure that you are constantly making progress towards your goal and will help keep you motivated and focused on the journey ahead.

Despite often facing tremendous adversity, some people are able to use their past experiences to create a better future for themselves. This is often accomplished through determination and resilience. Even in the face of seemingly insurmountable obstacles, these individuals are able to find the strength to push forward and make something positive out of their lives. Through hard work, dedication, and an unshakeable belief in themselves, these individuals are able to transform their futures from one defined by tragedy into one that is filled with hope and promise. By overcoming adversity, they show that anything is possible when you never give up on yourself.

Fear and laziness are two of the biggest obstacles we face when it comes to achieving our ambitions and goals. Fear can create a feeling of uncertainty, leading you to hesitate or even give up entirely. Similarly, laziness can cause you to procrastinate or put off the necessary steps needed to reach your goals. It is important to recognize these feelings for what they are and confront them head on. Remind yourself of why you are striving for your goal in the first place and take small steps each day towards achieving it. With determination and focus, nothing is out of reach!

Most people tend to consider what is possible and then decide what result they want to achieve. This can be a great way to stay focused and motivated in achieving your goals. When considering what is possible, it is important to think about the resources available, both internal and external. It may also be helpful to consider any potential obstacles that could stand in the way of success. Once you have a general idea of what is possible, you can then use this information to decide the outcome you would like to pursue. After determining the desired result, it can be useful to create a plan of action that outlines how you will reach your goal. By taking the time to consider all options and develop a plan for success, you can increase your chances of achieving the desired RESULTS. As an entrepreneur, it is important to have a clear understanding of what result you want to create with your business. Once you have identified the desired outcome, you can then begin to consider what processes and strategies are necessary for achieving that result. This

might involve researching the market, identifying potential customers, creating a marketing plan, or even setting up a business structure. By taking the time to consider what actions are required to achieve your desired result, you can ensure that your business is on the right path for success.

We all know that success in life or business largely depends on our ability to take initiative and push ourselves. No one else is going to do it for us. It requires us to take responsibility and make the effort necessary to bring about change. We must take action on our goals, dreams, and aspirations, as no one else can do that for us. By taking consistent actions towards our goals, we will have a greater chance of achieving them. To push yourself further, create a plan of action that outlines the steps you need to take and commit to following through with it. With dedication and perseverance we can achieve great things on our own terms!

The phrase "first you learn and then you remove the alphabet 'L'" is an expression used to emphasize the importance of learning before taking any action. It implies that knowledge should be acquired before attempting any task. This maxim serves as a reminder to take time to research, understand, or practice something before attempting it. Once the necessary knowledge has been acquired, then one can act with confidence knowing they have the proper skills and

understanding. The saying also acknowledges that not all tasks are equal, so it may be necessary to discard certain elements or approaches in order to complete an endeavor more effectively.

People who lack clarity in their lives, or who are unsure of their own goals and purpose, can often be a source of distraction and disruption. They may try to damage your focus or derail your progress in order to make themselves feel better about their own lack of direction. It is important to acknowledge these distractions, but not let them consume you. Instead, make it a priority to stay focused on your own goals and stay in control of your progress and success. By staying true to yourself, you will be able to achieve greater things and be less influenced by people who are unclear on what they want out of life.

People will always be quick to judge and criticize you, especially when it comes to trying new things or venturing into unfamiliar territory. It's important to remember that although their opinions may seem valid, they don't know the full story and may not have your best interests at heart. Additionally, there will always be people who actively try to stop you or bring you down in order to advance their own agenda. It is essential to keep your focus and maintain a clear vision of what you are trying to achieve, no matter

what obstacles people put in your way. Staying strong and believing in yourself is the key to success, so don't give up!

It can be hard to maintain a positive attitude when you're surrounded by people who don't like you. However, it's important to remember that your happiness is more powerful than their negativity and that it has the potential to kill off any negative feelings they may have towards you. By refusing to let their dislike get you down, and instead smiling and being content in their presence, you can have a profound impact on how they view you. Showing them that their opinions of you cannot dampen your spirits will drive home the point that they cannot control your emotions.

It is often said that our outlook on life can have a profound effect on our happiness. Looking at the world with a positive attitude can lead to a more fulfilling and rewarding life. On the other hand, having a negative mindset can drag us down and make life feel empty and unfulfilling. Practicing gratitude and focusing on the good in any situation can help us to shift our perspective and make us more aware of the positive aspects of our lives. Taking time for self-reflection, mindfulness, and meditation can also help us sharpen our focus and strengthen the connections between our mind, body, and soul. By making conscious decisions to look at the world from a place of positivity, we can open ourselves up to

increased joy, satisfaction.

We have all heard the phrase "work for a better tomorrow," but what does it really mean? It means that no matter how difficult the task at hand, we should always strive to make progress and improve our lives, both now and in the future. But when that better tomorrow actually arrives, instead of resting on our laurels, we must continue to push forward and work towards an even greater tomorrow. This is because progress never stops, and those who are willing to invest their time and effort into making the world a better place will reap the rewards of a brighter future. We can all do our part to help create a better tomorrow by never ceasing our efforts to make progress.

Life can sometimes be a struggle. We strive for success and aspire for a better tomorrow, but often forget about the joys of today. Instead of getting caught up in the hustle and bustle, why not take some time to enjoy the present? Life is full of special moments that should be savored and appreciated. So instead of focusing on what might be, let's take the time to enjoy what we have now. Let's live in the moment and appreciate all that life has to offer.

Time is a valuable commodity that, if not used and managed wisely, can easily be abused. It is important to recognize

that time is finite, and it is up to us to make the best of it. To use our time effectively, we should strive to set clear objectives and prioritize tasks accordingly. We should also strive to eliminate distractions and procrastination. Staying organized and disciplined will help ensure that we use our time in the best possible way, while avoiding its abuse. Ultimately, it's up to us how we spend our time – so let's make sure it counts!

Creating your own destiny and forging your own path is a process that requires time, effort and dedication. Life is about creating the best version of yourself and making the most out of opportunities that come your way. The decisions you make today shape who you will become tomorrow, so it's important to strive to become the person you want to be, no matter how difficult it may be. By creating goals and taking action to reach them, you can create a life full of meaning and purpose. The choices you make have the power to shape your life into something truly remarkable, so don't let anyone or anything stand in the way of creating your own destiny and forging your own path.

Reading great books can be a powerful tool for self-improvement and personal growth. Great books can open our minds to new ideas, challenge our perspectives, and encourage growth. They can also provide entertainment,

comfort, and companionship. Reading has been proven to reduce stress and anxiety by providing an escape from our day-to-day worries. The power of reading great books is undeniable; it can open your eyes to the beauty of the world around you, provide a much needed reprieve from your hectic life, and broaden your understanding of yourself and the world.

Education is much more than simply memorizing facts and figures. It is about developing the capacity to think critically, solve complex problems, and explore new avenues of knowledge. Education should foster creativity and imagination, helping students to explore their own interests and find innovative solutions. Furthermore, education should be tailored to individual needs, encouraging students to find their own unique paths in life. By striving to foster creativity and independent thinking, education can unlock the potential of each student's mind.

Education is an essential part of life, and should be seen as more than just a tool for memorizing facts and figures. Education can open up a world of possibilities and foster creativity due to the broad range of knowledge it provides. With education, you can expand your understanding of the world around you, and learn how to think strategically. Education gives you the power to see different angles and perspectives, enabling you to solve problems in creative ways. By learning new things, you can discover new paths that can lead to success. Education is meant not only to fill your mind with information but also to help make it more creative; instead of becoming a mere library of facts, education encourages creative thinking and exploration.

Finding hobbies that make you money, help you stay in shape and make you happy can be a challenge. However, with a bit of research and creativity, you can find three activities that give you everything you need. For the one to make money, look for opportunities like freelance writing or selling handmade items online. To stay fit, try something that gets your heart rate up like running or dancing. Finally, pick an

enjoyable activity such as gardening or listening to music that will bring joy and relaxation. With a combination of all three, you'll be sure to have all the benefits of each hobby without having to sacrifice any of them.

This saying is a reminder that no matter how bad things seem, we always have the strength and determination to come back from adversity. It encourages us to persevere, even when life throws us a curveball. The comeback is always stronger than the setback because it requires hard work and dedication to overcome difficulties. It also requires optimism, resilience, and self-belief in order to move past our struggles and achieve success. With this mindset, we can find the courage to never give up even when faced with the toughest of challenges. Therefore, "the comeback is always stronger than the setback" serves as an inspiring reminder that no matter what life throws at us, there is always hope for a brighter future.

Both winners and losers fail. It's a fact of life and something we all have to face at some point in our lives. The difference between the two, however, lies in their ability to pick themselves up and continue trying. The winners keep going no matter how many times they fail or face obstacles, while the losers often quit when things get tough. Winners refuse to accept defeat and have the strength and determination to

keep going until they succeed. This is why it is so important to never give up on your goals and dreams - success may be just around the corner!

When a child is learning how to walk, it can be a difficult and sometimes frustrating process. They may take many falls before they learn how to balance and stay upright. However, no matter how many times the child falls down, they never give up. They continue to try again and again until they eventually reach their goal. This can be seen as an analogy for life; no matter how many times we may fail or make mistakes, we should never give up and must keep trying no matter what. With patience and perseverance, we can eventually achieve success in whatever endeavor we pursue.

Changing your attitude and the way you view the world can have a profound effect on your life. It is all about how you choose to interpret situations, people, and events. When approaching things with an open mind and a positive attitude, you can often find solutions that were not previously considered. Additionally, choosing to stay positive can help to reduce stress and anxiety. With a more optimistic outlook, it is easier to focus on solutions rather than dwelling on problems. By changing your attitude and the way you see things in life, you can open up a world of

possibilities.

It can be hard to do what is best for yourself, especially when it goes against what other people want. However, it's important to remember that you have the right and responsibility to make decisions that are in your best interest. It can be difficult to stand up for yourself and resist peer pressure, but that is part of being an adult. When faced with tough decisions, focus on what will make you happiest in the long run - don't let anyone step on your dreams! Doing what is best for you, as harsh as it sounds, can help you lead a more fulfilling life.

Reading is an essential part of a healthy lifestyle, as it provides nourishment for the mind in much the same way that exercise does for the body. A single good book can have a transformative effect on your life, causing you to think differently and see the world in a new light. Reading also has numerous other benefits, including providing entertainment and improving critical thinking skills. Additionally, reading can improve concentration, help you process and retain information better, and even reduce stress. By taking the time to read regularly, you can reap these rewards and more.

Everyone experiences tough times in life, and it can feel like a storm has arrived to disrupt everything. However, it is important to remember that not all storms are set out to destroy us. In fact, some stormy times can be seen as an opportunity for growth and progress. The challenge of a difficult situation can open up new possibilities and pathways that may not have been available before. It is helpful to remember that not all storms come to ruin our lives; sometimes they come to clear our path and make room for something better.

It is easy to get caught up in the mundane tasks of life: paying bills, going to work, and doing everyday activities. However, life is much more than that. Everyone is born with unique gifts, talents, and passions and it is our responsibility to use them to create a meaningful life. By pursuing our passions and striving for excellence we can find purpose and fulfillment in life that goes beyond just getting by. So don't be content with just paying bills and dying; use your gifts to live an extraordinary life!

It's easy to underestimate the importance of having a strong mental approach when it comes to achieving success. No matter what your goals are, it will always come down to how you think and how you believe in yourself. To achieve success, you need to have faith that you can reach your goals and be willing to put in the work necessary to get there. One of the biggest obstacles you'll face is overcoming negative self-talk and replacing it with positive affirmations. That's why it's so important to take time each day for reflection and take steps towards building a mindset that believes in yourself and your capabilities. With some patience and focus, you can start to form new habits and attitudes that will lead you towards success.

The phrase, "Don't be afraid of being outnumbered. Eagles fly alone. Pigeons flock together" is a powerful reminder of the importance of standing firm in one's convictions even if it means going against the majority. This quote highlights that although safety can be found in numbers, strength and courage can be found in standing alone. It encourages individuals to have the confidence to go against what is popular and make their own path. The message here is clear: don't be afraid to stand out from the crowd and pursue your own goals - it is often more rewarding than conforming to societal standards.

A 20-year-old should invest in their future, and this starts with investing in education, job or business and great relationships. Education can open doors to better opportunities later down the line and is an important building block for a successful career. Investing time into finding a job or starting a business gives you structure and helps to create financial security. Finally, building strong relationships is key to having both personal and professional success. Investing in these key areas now will pay off in the long run!

Finding your passion can be a daunting task, but it's worth the effort. Taking the time to try new things and explore your interests is essential if you want to discover something that truly resonates with you. It could be something as simple as trying out a new hobby or signing up for an online course. It could also mean getting out of your comfort zone and meeting new people in different fields. By taking these steps, you'll be able to expand your horizons and open yourself up to the possibility of finding something that will make you truly passionate.

Finding your passion is the first step towards achieving success. It is important to have a clear idea of what you want to do and why you want to do it. Once you have identified your passion, living below your means is essential in order to save money and invest in yourself. Having a mentor can help guide you on the right path and provide support when things get tough. Once all of these steps have been taken, the next step is to start a business. This requires planning, research, and hard work, but with the right mindset and dedication it is possible to achieve success.

Before you turn 30, it is important to have a plan for your future. Working hard and becoming financially independent should be at the top of your list. This means budgeting for savings, investing in stocks and bonds, and setting aside money for retirement. Additionally, this may involve taking on extra work or starting a side business to increase your income and savings. Becoming financially independent before 30 will help you to secure your future and give you the freedom to pursue your dreams without worry. Reading a lot, surrounding yourself with leaders, being different and developing multiple streams of income are all powerful strategies for success. Reading is a great way to learn about different topics, gain new perspectives and develop your skills. Surrounding yourself with strong leaders can help you to stay motivated and focused on the goals you want to achieve. Being different and standing out from the crowd can help you to find success by offering something unique from what everyone else is doing. Finally, diversifying your income allows you to hedge against risk and build a reliable financial foundation for yourself. Incorporating these strategies into your daily routine can help set you up for

long-term success.

It can be disheartening to feel like you're not being heard or respected. Whether you're at the bottom, middle, or top of the corporate ladder, it's important to remember that everyone deserves respect. People who don't give it to you at the bottom may ignore you in the middle and then try to take credit for your accomplishments at the top. It's important to stay true to yourself and make sure that your voice is heard, no matter where you are in an organization. Speak up and don't let anyone take away from your hard work and dedication.

Once you get used to the ease and convenience that comfort provides, it can be difficult to give it up. Comfort can become an addiction, as many people tend to seek out comfort in their daily lives. Comfort can provide a sense of security and stability, which can be especially attractive when there is so much uncertainty in the world. This craving for comfort can manifest itself in many different ways, such as seeking out familiar foods or activities, or even buying items that provide short-term pleasure or joy. Ultimately, once you become accustomed to comfort, it can be hard to live without it.
The idea that a weak man, given a comfortable life would be content to abandon his ambitions and settle into complacency is a commonly held one. It presupposes that

the individual in question lacks the ambition or strength of will necessary to pursue their goals when faced with the prospect of easy living. This may be true in some cases, but it is important to remember that many people are capable of thriving even in difficult circumstances. With proper support and motivation, a weak man can still strive for his goals and dreams, no matter what life throws at him.

Money is being transferred around the world every hour, every minute, every second, and every day. From online transfers to international payments, money moves through an intricate network of banks and financial institutions in order to reach its destination. The speed of these transactions is incredible, with some payments taking only seconds to process. This helps to facilitate global business and make international trade faster and easier than ever before. By increasing the speed of money transfers, we can open up new possibilities in our interconnected world. Helping people solve problems is a great way to engage and connect with your audience. With the right approach, you can show them that you are an expert in your field and provide valuable solutions to their needs. When it comes to identifying problems, they can range from practical issues such as needing a new car tire or a DIY project gone wrong, to lifestyle issues such as weight loss or financial planning. By understanding the problem and providing helpful solutions, you can create content that resonates with your audience and encourages them to come back for more.

It is often said that a confused mind creates problems where none exist, while a focused and clear mind can tackle every problem that comes its way. When we are overwhelmed with too much information or too many tasks, our minds become cluttered and confused. This leads to overthinking and worrying about unnecessary details that can prevent us from making progress on our goals. On the other hand, when we take the time to focus on the task at hand, break it down into manageable steps, and remain mindful of our intentions, it becomes much easier to stay on track and make tangible progress. A focused mind helps us to prioritize our efforts and be more productive.

It is all too easy to become complacent and allow potential to remain merely potential. In order to achieve any sort of success, it is necessary to take action in order to make the most of that potential. This can be difficult, especially when it involves stepping out of one's comfort zone, but without taking action, one's potential will remain just that—potential. It is only by working hard, setting goals and taking risks that one can make the most of their potential and achieve real results. Every great accomplishment begins with small steps towards a goal, and these steps have to be taken in order for success to be achieved.

It is often said that our most valuable asset is our ability to think differently. In a world full of conformity and sameness, it is important to be able to stand out and think in new and creative ways. Those who can do this are able to see the world from different perspectives, understand complex problems, and come up with innovative solutions. This can often help them achieve success in their careers that may otherwise have been out of reach. Being able to think differently will always be an asset no matter what field you work in or what challenges life throws at you.

A man with a hustle needs a woman who can share his passions and help him achieve his goals. A woman with a vision is someone who can provide him with the support, encouragement, and guidance he needs to reach success. She will also be able to listen to him, understand his ideas and offer her own input when necessary. On the other hand, a little girl who parties may not be able to offer such support or have the same level of commitment and dedication that is required for success. It is important for a man with a hustle to find someone who shares his vision, passion and determination in order to help him attain his ambitions.

It can be easy to become comfortable with who we are, and to accept ourselves as we are without trying to grow or become better versions of ourselves. However, this attitude can lead us to miss out on many opportunities for personal growth and development. If we don't strive to become who we could be, then we are sacrificing a great potential that lies within us. We should strive to reach our highest potential while still being true to our core values and principles. By challenging ourselves and pushing our boundaries, we can reach greater heights and live more fulfilling lives.

People often hide their feelings of envy and resentment behind a facade of laughter. They may feel intimidated by someone's success or accomplishments, or even resentful of the attention that person receives. To avoid confronting their own insecurities, they may try to make light of the situation through jokes or mocking remarks. Unfortunately, this type of behavior only serves to hurt rather than heal. It is important to recognize these negative feelings and find healthy ways to work through them, rather than masking them with humor.

Finding the right person to be in a relationship with is always important. The wrong person can distract you from achieving your goals and potentially lead to unhappiness.

On the other hand, the right person can provide motivation, support, and understanding to help you achieve your ambitions. A successful relationship involves both parties working together to reach common goals. When it comes to relationships, it's essential to find someone who will have your back and motivate you towards success. While the wrong girl may provide short-term satisfaction, it's essential to look for someone who will help bring out your best self and propel you towards greatness in the long run.

The person you will be in five years depends largely on the books you read and the people you surround yourself with. Reading is a great way to expose yourself to a variety of ideas, opinions, and perspectives. By opening yourself up to these different points of view, you can learn more about yourself and the world around you. Additionally, surrounding yourself with positive people who challenge and inspire you can help to propel your personal growth over time. Ultimately, it is up to you to decide what kind of person you want to become in five years. By engaging in activities that are aligned with this vision, such as reading inspiring books and connecting with like-minded individuals, you can create conditions for success that will help make your goals a reality.

It can be easy to fall into a victim mentality, feeling like life is out of your control or that you have no power to make change. However, it is important to take ownership of our lives and look for ways to create positive change. Rather than being a passive observer in your own life, work to identify areas where you can make a difference and take action. It may not be easy, but it's always worth the effort. By breaking down the problem into smaller steps and tackling them one by one, you can break free from the victim mentality and create real change in your life.

McDonald's is now taking advantage of a new form of advertisement with environmental graffiti! This form of advertising uses graffiti to paint messages on walls in public places. These messages can range from slogans to pictures, promoting the brand and its products in an environmentally friendly manner. Not only does this technique provide free advertising, but it also sends a message that McDonald's is committed to green initiatives. By leveraging environmental graffiti, McDonald's is able to create buzz around its brand while helping the environment at the same time.

If Jeff Bezos had given up after his first attempt at running an online business, the world would be without one of the most successful entrepreneurs of all time. Jeff Bezos started Zshops in 1995 as an online auction site but it ultimately

failed. Despite this failure, Bezos persevered with his online venture and eventually created Amazon.com in 1997. This new company revolutionized how people shop online and today it is considered one of the largest companies in the world. Bezos' resilience and refusal to give up despite early failures is an inspiring example to other entrepreneurs and a testament to the belief that success comes through hard work and dedication.

Had J.K. Rowling given up after being turned down by multiple publishers for years, the world would have been denied the beloved Harry Potter series. But, instead of giving up, she persevered and eventually found a publisher who believed in her vision and was willing to take a chance on her writing. Her success serves as an inspiring reminder that sometimes our path to success is not linear and that perseverance can be rewarded in unexpected ways.

If Bill Gates had given up after his first software company, "Traf-o-data", failed, he would have missed out on creating one of the world's most successful and profitable corporations – Microsoft. Despite the failure of his first venture, Bill Gates persevered and continued to pursue his passion for technology. This led to the creation of a number of software companies that eventually formed the basis for Microsoft. It is through this determination and resilience that Gates was able to achieve success in business, becoming one of the world's wealthiest individuals in the process. His story serves as an inspiring example of what is possible when we don't give up on our dreams.

If Howard Shultz had given up after the 242nd bank turned him down, he wouldn't have had the opportunity to revolutionize Starbucks and lead them to become a multi-billion dollar company. Rejection is a part of any entrepreneur's journey, but it's important not to let it deter you from achieving your goals. Shultz used each rejection as an opportunity to learn and grow, and eventually he found *success in his endeavors. His story serves as a reminder that no matter how many obstacles you face, it's possible to reach your dreams if you never give up.*

If Walt Disney had given up after his theme park concept was trashed 302 times, the world would have been deprived of one of its most iconic companies. Walt Disney's perseverance in the face of rejection taught us that with hard work and dedication, anything is possible. He took a risk and followed his vision, despite being told no by nearly everyone he pitched to. His unwavering drive to make his dream come true ultimately resulted in the creation of Disneyland, a place where children and adults can escape reality and explore an exciting world of fantasy and imagination. Walt Disney's story is a reminder that with dedication, anything is possible.

The odds of becoming the next Elon Musk and creating the next SpaceX are incredibly low. Despite Musk's incredible success, it is highly unlikely that anyone else will achieve the same level of success. The reality is that achieving such a feat requires significant resources, time, and dedication. Moreover, there are numerous unknown variables that could prevent someone from achieving similar levels of success. Therefore, it is important to recognize the remarkable achievement of Elon Musk and acknowledge that most people simply cannot replicate his success.

It can be easy to doubt ourselves, but believing in ourselves and pursuing our passions is a key part of leading a fulfilling life. Even when the odds are against us, we can find strength within ourselves to overcome any obstacle. It's important to remember that passion is contagious - if we believe in ourselves, it will likely inspire those around us to do the same. So, no matter how difficult your chosen path may seem, always believe in yourself and chase your passion. Doing so will open up a world of possibilities that you never knew existed.

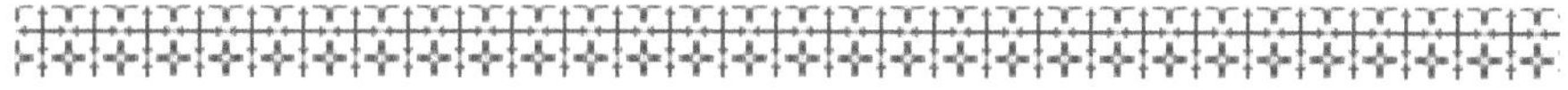

When a man asked an artist how they could create such stunning works of art out of stone, the artist replied that it was all about passion. They explained that if you have a true appreciation for the stone's natural beauty, you can find ways to bring out its unique characteristics and create something beautiful. The artist also shared their insight into how different tools, from chisels and hammers to sandpaper, can be used to shape and refine the stone's texture. Through this combination of skill, craftsmanship, and creativity, the artist is able to transform a seemingly ordinary piece of rock into an extraordinary work of art.

Your happiness is a state of mind that you create for yourself. It is not something that can be found outside of yourself, but rather through mindful practices and inner reflections. Removing worry is a key factor in creating a state of contentment and joy. This can be accomplished by recognizing your thoughts and beliefs, and then consciously making an effort to shift them in more positive directions. When we let go of our worries, we open ourselves up to the possibility of finding true happiness within ourselves.

www.ingramcontent.com/pod-product-compliance
Lightning Source LLC
Chambersburg PA
CBHW071435130726
47997CB00006B/2094